W9-APT-176

ALSO BY SARAH RUDEN

TRANSLATIONS

Vergil: The Aeneid

The Homeric Hymns

Aristophanes: Lysistrata

Petronius: Satyricon

ORIGINAL POETRY

Other Places

PAUL AMONG THE PEOPLE

PAUL AMONG THE PEOPLE

THE APOSTLE REINTERPRETED AND REIMAGINED IN HIS OWN TIME

SARAH RUDEN

PANTHEON BOOKS
NEW YORK

Pantheon Books and colophon are registered trademarks of Random House, Inc.

Grateful acknowledgment is made to the following for permission to reprint previously published material:
Hackett Publishing Company, Inc.: Excerpts from *Homeric Hymns,* translated by Sarah Ruden, copyright © 2005 by Hackett Publishing Company, Inc. (Indianapolis: Hackett Publishing Company, 2005); excerpts from *Lysistrata* by Aristophanes, translated by Sarah Ruden, copyright © 2003 by Hackett Publishing Company, Inc. (Indianapolis: Hackett Publishing Company, 2003); and excerpts from *Satyricon* by Petronius, translated by Sarah Ruden, copyright © 2000 by Hackett Publishing Company, Inc. (Indianapolis: Hackett Publishing Company, 2000). All rights reserved. Reprinted by permission of Hackett Publishing Company, Inc.
Yale University Press: Excerpts from *The Aeneid* by Vergil, translated by Sarah Ruden, copyright © 2008 by Yale University. Reprinted by permission of Yale University Press.

Library of Congress Cataloging-in-Publication Data
Ruden, Sarah.
Paul among the people : The Apostle reinterpreted and reimagined in his own time / Sarah Ruden.
p. cm.
Includes bibliographical references (p.).
ISBN 978-0-375-42501-1
1. Bible. N.T. Epistles of Paul—Theology. 2. Paul, the Apostle, Saint.
I. Title.
BS2651.R83 2010
225.9'2—dc22 2009020969

www.pantheonbooks.com

Printed in the United States of America

First Edition

2 4 6 8 9 7 5 3 1

FOR
THE LATE PROFESSOR W. V. CLAUSEN,
MY TEACHER

You, by the window here with me,
Who never spoke to me before,
But called me in
When I went by your office door,

You are a stranger—
Why insist I see
What stands below your window there,
The white tree?

The spring went by like a dull rain
Of "It is gone," "You cannot have it,"
"We will have to see,"
And then you showed me this,
The glittering tree,

Which stands out in an open place,
For anyone at all to see,
And now I am that anyone,
Since when he looks, he looks for love of me,
And I for love of him,
At the flowering tree.

It is so hard to say, so plain to see.
But you have made it speak, it speaks through me:
The vivid tree.

CONTENTS

ACKNOWLEDGMENTS

Thanks abound, for spiritual, scholarly, and practical help: to David and Marjorie Ball, Marcelle Martin, and Ken and Katharine Jacobsen at Pendle Hill Quaker Study Center; to Sheila Murnaghan and the Classics Department at the University of Pennsylvania; to my agents, Glen Hartley and Lynn Chu; to Yale Divinity School—I was a stranger, and you took me in; to Leslie Williams—hungry, and you fed me; and to George and Sadie Stegmann, Caro Attwell, and Tom Conroy—*ni me plus oculis vestris amaretis.*

PREFACE: WHO WAS PAUL?

Probably around a decade after the birth of Christ, the person who would become the most important exponent of Christianity was born. Paul belonged to a Jewish family in the port city of Tarsus (on the southern coast of what is now Turkey), in the Roman province of Cilicia. He was originally called Saul, the name of a king in the Hebrew Bible, but as a missionary of the new sect he adopted the name of Roman origin by which he is still commonly known, sometimes with the addition of the title "saint" or "the apostle."*

Paul was a native or early Greek speaker, and all of his surviving writings are in that language. According to Acts of the Apostles (the New Testament book that recounts events after those in the four gospels), he was fluent in Hebrew as well (Acts 21:40; 22:20). How much Latin he knew is uncertain. Acts shows him dealing suavely with Roman officials, but

*The Greek transliteration of the Hebrew name "Saul" means "man with a mincing, queeny walk," clearly not ideal for a proselytizer among Greek speakers, but there may have been some other reason for the name change.

many Romans read and spoke Greek, the business language of the entire Mediterranean.

Tarsus had come under the Greek Seleucid empire more than 250 years before falling to the Romans in the early first century B.C. It was a cosmopolitan city: as almost everywhere, the Greeks and Romans had overridden all previous hegemonies (which in this case were Hittite, Assyrian, and Persian). Tarsus was known for commerce, for the same kind of oratorical and philosophical higher education enjoyed at Athens and Rome, and for its cult of Hercules. It had all of the public works of any established Roman provincial capital, including monumental temples, a stadium, and a sophisticated water supply.

Since Paul was a tent maker, and since trades were usually passed on through families, it is safe to assume that this was the family business. It is a tricky question whether he was a Roman citizen. This would not have been odd for a provincial from a respectable family. But if Paul had been born a citizen, as Acts testifies (22:27–28), why did he only once—and only quite late, after years of submitting to official beatings and ad hoc imprisonment—invoke his privilege of due process ending at Rome? Perhaps it was one thing to be a Roman citizen, another to rely on citizenship amid the touchy religious and cultural politics he had to negotiate. Since he does not seem to have traveled with the usual entourage (including slaves) of a man of position, it would have been easy to assume he was *not* a Roman citizen.

Even more confusing, this cultured and influential man, who never questioned his own prerogatives as a leader, supported himself at times by crafting tents with his own hands. And—of course—what about the strange religion he was aggressively spreading? His legal status must have been only one question in people's minds as they tried to work out who he was, what he was up to, and how to react to him.

As a young man, Paul went to Jerusalem for Jewish religious purposes, and by his own account he was a Pharisee (Philippians 3:5). This group was concerned with ritual purity, especially in and around the Temple. Marriage was prescribed for such men, but there is no telling whether Paul ever had a wife or children.

While in Jerusalem, he became an agent of the Temple in attacking the recently crucified Jesus' followers, who were playing a disruptive and precarious role within Judaism. On the road to Damascus with documents authorizing a purge in that city, he heard the voice of Jesus rebuking him, was blinded, and recovered to be baptized and slowly work his way into the new movement (Acts 9ff.; Galatians 1:13–24).

The full history of his missions is uncertain, though scholars have worked out several more or less plausible timelines. Acts summarizes his career, gives versions of some of his sermons, and takes a particular (and probably anti-Jewish) interest in how often and how badly he got into trouble. But the author of Acts is sometimes only copying a memoir or journal, not even changing the word "we" to "they." Paul's letters are more detailed than Acts, but most of the time he either focuses on an individual community's problems (spiritual or practical) or preaches the new faith. Paul's accounts of his own activities are never profuse.

It is clear, however, that he made at least three long missionary journeys, going farther to the west over time. He made as many as five trips back to Jerusalem, the center of Christianity at the time. (Not that any followers of Jesus were calling themselves "Christians" yet: the term started as a taunt, perhaps best translated as "the hyped-up fans/

political mob of 'the Anointed One'" [Acts 11:26], and the single time Paul is shown being teased with it, he demurs humorously [Acts 26:28–29].) Meetings there included the Jerusalem Conference, probably in 49 or 50 B.C., where Paul received from the leaders of the new sect the authority to evangelize non-Jews. Later, in Antioch, he nevertheless clashed with Jesus' disciple Peter, who he claimed was hypocritically opposing the agreed-upon policy of tolerance and inclusion. But Paul was never a favorite at Jerusalem. He was not as credible there as Jesus' surviving companions and relatives; he may have failed ever to win trust, because of his early persecutions; and his letters suggest that at best he was not easy to get along with.

His final arrest among many came around 57 A.D. in Jerusalem, where he had arrived with charitable donations but found his relations with both Jews and Christians still poor. He appealed to Rome and remained jailed, under guard during transport or under house arrest until as late as 65 A.D., a date that would allow us to attribute his death to the first great persecution of Christians, by the emperor Nero, who blamed them for the great fire of 64 A.D. There is no good evidence of the journey to Spain he was planning to make after his time in Rome (Romans 15:24–28).

In spite of all this, Paul was the man who did the most to create the Christian church after the brief, otherworldly ministry of Jesus. He established, guided, and advised a number of religious assemblies in Asia Minor, Greece, and Italy. Though Peter, James the brother of Jesus, and John were the three other most important leaders of the sect, Acts spends relatively little time on any of them (and they did not write the New Testament books attributed to them). Paul appears already in Acts 7, and from chapter 13 to the end, at chapter 28, he is the protagonist.

Acts (along with the gospel of Luke) is ascribed (though not without controversy) to Luke, the "beloved physician" and friend of Paul, but it cannot be favoritism alone that gives Paul such a crucial role. Paul's churches were the prototype in Europe, where Christianity held fast, becoming and staying dominant.

Paul was also crucial as an author. Uniquely in the Bible, he is like a Greco-Roman or modern expository writer, a definite historical person writing down his own thoughts and experiences under his own name and on his own responsibility. He sent exhortations and instructions to Christian communities, and some of these "letters to" or "epistles to" survive. Romans, 1 and 2 Corinthians, Galatians, Philippians, 1 Thessalonians, and Philemon are the ones attributed to him with little or no scholarly doubt, and they make up seven out of twenty-seven books in the New Testament. (The seven letters that many, or most, modern scholars say have been falsely attributed to him—2 Thessalonians, Colossians, Ephesians, 1 and 2 Timothy, Titus, and Hebrews—are a further measure of his influence: his was the most authoritative name under which to put early Christian treatises.)

Because Paul died before 66 A.D., the letters are earlier than the earliest canonical gospel, Mark. The work biblical scholars hypothetically reconstruct under the name Q, a collection of sayings of Jesus, may have existed during Paul's lifetime, as well as other extant books about Jesus (such as the gospel of Thomas) that did not make it into the Bible. If so, Paul most likely did not use them. He makes almost no reference to Jesus' life apart from the crucifixion episode, and he quotes Jesus directly and by name only in 1 Corinthians 11:23–25, in narrating the Last Supper.

Paul climbed to this lonely and towering position the hard way. There were other wide-ranging missionaries claiming authority from Jesus, with other agenda. Paul won.

The most controversial issue during his time as a missionary was the new sect's relationship to the Jewish covenant. Were Christianity and Judaism basically the same thing? In that case, then circumcision and the observance of strict dietary laws were essential for belonging, and the new strain of the old religion would draw most of its authority from Jerusalem and the Temple—and have limited appeal. Greeks and Romans considered circumcision a mutilation, and Jews were forbidden even to eat alongside non-Jews. The synagogues of the Diaspora drew many gentile "God-fearers" or "God-worshippers," but for them to become full Jews would have meant a "maiming" operation and isolation within their own households and cities. Paul had to insist that Judaism was not a gatekeeper to Christianity. But for pious Jews, the idea of the Jew Jesus starting a movement that negated any part of the Law was abominable.

Yet the very existence of the God-fearers and God-worshippers implies an advantage Paul had as a Jew well schooled in his tradition: he understood the lure of monotheism and of a consistently just and merciful God unlike any of the deities of the Greco-Roman pantheon; and he knew the beauty of a deeply orderly community, such as polytheistic ideology had never managed to produce. Paul sensed that the practices of the scorned, harried Jews would not be attracting any gentiles who did not experience their own religion as cynical and their own society as brutal.

Perhaps the greatest irony about his letters is that, in the passages modern readers consider most intolerant, Paul seems, on an examination in context, to be addressing this brutality most humanely. The Greeks and Romans deified materialism in the form of idolatry, and they deified violence and exploitation through their belief that these were the ways the gods operated. Paul fought this ideology and all of its manifestations. Rather than repressing women, slaves, or homosexuals, he made—for his time—progressive rules for the inclusion of all of them in the Christian community, drawing on (but not limited by) traditional Jewish ethics.

At the same time, Paul was from a sophisticated port city, where he had grown up in a commercial family and studied rhetoric and philosophy as any privileged Greek or Roman youth would. He knew the Greeks' and Romans' longing, best expressed in a number of mystery cults, for a personally persuasive explanation of the meaning of life. Judaism did not offer this.

Paul had something new to offer everyone: the idea of salvation through Jesus' death and resurrection. According to Paul, God, out of love, had sent his Son to suffer and die in order to pull humans out of their human state and beyond all suffering and death.

His special experience helped make him perhaps the greatest theological genius of all time. On the Damascus road, he was confronted by the full horror of his human limitations. "Saul, Saul, why do you persecute me?" the voice asked (Acts 9:4). He conceived that by persecuting human beings, he was persecuting God himself. God did not live in the Temple (the Christian preacher Stephen had claimed that he didn't—just before Paul assisted at the young man's stoning [Acts 7:44–50, 8:1]), and his essence was not rules and institutions. He lived within humanity, so that any hurt done to them—like the hurt done to Jesus in human form—was an assault on God.

But an even stranger idea appears to have emerged from Paul's healing through a follower of Jesus, Ananias (Acts 9:10–19). The answer for human beings, who in their imperfect state were selfish, stupid, and always helplessly hurting one another, was neither a desperate effort to be righteous nor an acceptance that a righteous God would punish them; they must instead learn that God had unlimited compassion and would save them. This was a *charis,* or free gift ("grace" is the rather esoteric-sounding modern translation), a loving power and presence during life and an assurance of eternal life. If this all seems to be explicit in the gospels, it is probably because it was written back into these later documents. The evidence is strong that the full Christian doctrine came not from Jesus' mouth but from Paul's pen.

Baptism marked the acceptance of salvation, and a life useful to the community testified to a true conversion. The faith-versus-works debate shown in the letter of James (and of huge importance in the later history of Christianity) may have exercised some Christians, but not Paul. To his mind, faith automatically caused believers to do their best. If a community was conspicuously sinful or troubled, it must renew its faith. There was no vital division between people's trust in God and their actions, however imperfect either might be; the one could not be sincere and therefore acceptable without the other's being the same, though trust in God came first, since the divine always preceded the human.

But Paul urged his followers not to worry too much about metaphysics: God would simply meet them in their prayers, not halfway but all the way, with whatever help they truly needed, teaching them to rejoice in their very weakness in relation to the divine.

Paul himself, while never overcoming his faults, drew great strength from his faith. The letter to Philemon, for example, written in prison, about a runaway slave who has become a Christian and thrown himself on Paul's protection (as if imprisonment had not been enough to deal with), is full of inside jokes and high-as-a-kite invocations of the transcendent. A slave was, in Greek or Roman eyes, absolutely limited as to the consideration anyone (even a god) could show for him. Even if freed, he would always be treated as a social, civic, and spiritual inferior. A runaway had no right to any consideration at all. Deploying Christian ideas against Greco-Roman culture, Paul joyfully mocks the notion that any person placing himself in the hands of God can be limited or degraded in any way that matters. The letter must represent the most fun anyone ever had writing while incarcerated.

The letter to Philemon may be the most explicit demonstration of how, more than anyone else, Paul created the Western individual human being, unconditionally precious to God and therefore entitled to the consideration of other human beings. There is no sign that Paul intended all the social change that gradually (and sometimes traumatically) resulted, the development of the rights and freedoms that characterize the West. He laid down the law against only the worst abuses, such as pederasty, male promiscuity, and forced marriage. But broad social change did follow inevitably from the idea he spread: that God's love was sublime and infinite, yet immediately knowable to everyone. No other intellect contributed as much to making us who we are.

This book is an attempt to get further inside Paul's world and, through this, to understand him better.

PAUL AMONG THE PEOPLE

CHAPTER 1: PAUL AND ARISTOPHANES—NO, REALLY

The last thing I expected my Greek and Latin to be of any use for was a better understanding of Paul. The very idea, had anyone proposed it, would have annoyed me. I am a Christian, but like many, I kept Paul in a pen out back with the louder and more sexist Old Testament prophets. Jesus was my teacher; Paul was an embarrassment.

But one day, in a Bible study class I was taking, a young woman objected to the stricture against sorcery in the "fruit of the Spirit" passage in Paul's letter to the Galatians. She said that to her sorcery meant "just the ability to project my power and essence." Most of the class gave the familiar sigh: Paul *was* kind of a brute, wasn't he? I would have sighed too, had there not flashed into my mind an example of what sorcery could mean in a Greco-Roman context: the Roman poet Horace's image of a small boy buried up to his neck and left to starve to death while staring at food, so that his liver and bone marrow, which must now be imbued with his frenzied longing, could serve as a love charm. Paul, I reflected, may never have read this poem (which depicts a crime that may never have happened), but it shows the kind of reputation sorcery had in the Roman Empire—certainly among people with a polytheistic background, who made up the main readership for his letters both during his lifetime and after it. I could not get away from the thought that what his writings would have meant for them is probably as close as we can come to their basic original importance, as key documents (prior even to the gospels) inspiring the world-changing new movement, Christianity.

As I began to read Paul in connection to Greco-Roman writing, I seemed to be actually reading him: understanding his devotion and his constraints, and not simply listening to 1 Corinthians 13 with boredom and irritation, and with smug agreement to excoriations of his "betrayal of Jesus' message." I came to see how a man whom a divinity student friend of mine called "grumpy-pants Paul" had spread an uncompromising message of love, and how he had established a community that proved to have, if not a steady power for good, then at least a steady power for renewing its ideals. More and more, I wanted to take his part.

This feeling grew even stronger when I researched the origins of our bad impressions of Paul. It seemed that many reactions to him across the centuries had been distorted or incomplete in ways that would not have survived a look at his main contemporary and near-contemporary audiences through their own books. For every implausible reading of Paul, there were Greco-Roman works through the lens of which he showed more plausibly. The contrast between distant views of Paul in a variety of modern authors and the very near view that we can re-create came to seem like a way to organize a book.

Others have written defenses of Paul, but he needs—and deserves—all the help he can get. His faults are obvious enough: his bad temper, his self-righteousness, his anxiety. But we tend not to feel inspired that such a painfully human personality was able to achieve so much in the name of God. And we do not ask the obvious question, which is, what was he doing right in substance that is hidden from us under his manner? He must have been doing a great deal right or he could not have succeeded as he did.

And understanding his success is vital for letting him help us now. Paul dealt with several social issues that remain painful today. Read in a way that shows the challenges, ideals, and strategies behind his words, he usually offers diverse people something they can agree on. In the case of homosexuality, it is the passion he had for ending exploitative sex, the only physical expression of homoeroticism he likely knew about. Getting closer to Paul as he really was can allow Christians and non-Christians either to find common ground to build on or to part ways more peacefully, because they see that they merely disagree on how to reach the same goals and can no longer call each other's intentions evil.

Paul is, of course, not easy to understand. Probably many Greeks and Romans themselves misunderstood him or skimmed the surface of his arguments when he used terms such as "law" (referring to the Jewish religious law in which he himself was trained). But their literature is still a good basis for interpretation: they shared a language with him, Greek, and a cosmopolitan urban culture, that of the Roman Empire, and he considered evangelizing them his special mission.

What Greco-Roman works can teach about Paul's writings is incredibly rich and virtually unexplored so far—and often rather mortifying to a previous knee-jerk anti-Paulist like me. For example, there is the matter of the *kōmos* and the right to have a really good party. The "fruit of the Spirit" passage in Galatians does not forbid "carousing," the outrageous New Revised Standard Version translation of the word, or "revellings," as in the King James. A *kōmos* was a late-night, very drunken, sometimes violent postparty parade—which could even end in kidnapping and rape. We have vivid scenes of it in Greek comedy and other genres. It was nearly the worst of Greek nightlife, and if any Christian young men counted on still being allowed to behave like rampaging frat boys or overgrown trick-or-treaters in a foul mood, their elders would have been relieved to have it in writing from Paul that this was banned. Other translations, probably in an effort to be less dour, have "orgies," but that is unsatisfactory: some features of Greek parties *were* orgylike, but not the *kōmos.* And since orgies are quite rare today (I think), a reader might wonder why Paul included something so unusual in his list, as if a modern pastor were to speak against flashing. We would never guess from the English that the abuse Paul is speaking of is *both* serious and customary.

I was at first puzzled that nobody had lined up Paul's letters and Greco-Roman literature in any systematic way before, but I soon realized that scholarly disciplines are not set up for it. In seven years at Harvard as a classics graduate student, I got to know exactly two divinity students, and only as friends, not as scholars. I never met any of the divinity professors, wherever they were, somewhere up in the cloudy regions of the North Yard. Their language courses were separate, and in my curriculum there was not a single piece of Christian literature out of all that belonged to the era I was studying. We behaved as if the New Testament had not been written in Greek, as if Paul had not been a Hellenized Jew and by some accounts a Roman citizen, and as if the

Roman Empire at its greatest period of power had not been in the early Christians' background.

I was now stunned at how much perspective this took away from Christianity. "Oh, yeah, we're not supposed to have orgies, no kidding." Maybe shallowness of perspective is one reason so many people consider the religion passé—not interesting, not inspiring, not useful. To me, even the first efforts at setting Paul's words against the words of polytheistic authors helped explain why early Christianity was so compelling, growing as no popular movement ever had before. And as I went on, I found that—almost creepily—the passages to which the modern world has the most resistance were all telling me the same thing: contemporary readers would likely not have seen Paul's "authoritarian" policies as anything but ways to connect with one another in conscientious tenderness.

In this way, I was dragged away from a quite dear prejudice: that the socially concerned church was an invention of the modern era. (We Quakers have always thought our own sect invented it, but I won't go into that.) In fact, the compassionate community was there at the beginning, and its founder was Paul of Tarsus. To those asking, "But how do we live, right here, right now?" his answer was always in essence the same: "In a way worthy of God's infinite love for each of you."

This is his story as told not only by himself, but by Aristophanes, Herodas, Petronius, Juvenal, Apuleius, and many others he never met. It is the story of his challenges and his triumphs in their world. And here's a little of what it tells us for today.

CHAPTER 2: THE END OF FUN? PAUL AND PLEASURE

What was Paul's real message about the body and social life? Don't ask the Puritans.

When these gained power and sought to wipe out the enjoyments (games, drama, feasting, dancing, fancy hats) that the medieval church had spared, the main New Testament authority they alleged was Paul. Richard Baxter (1615–91) of Kidderminster, in England, cites him over and over in part VII of his *Directions to Weak Christians,* "Directions Against the Master Sin; Sensuality, Flesh-Pleasing, or Voluptuousness." By this time, "flesh" meant roughly anything that is often done for its own sake, like eating or conversation, and Baxter condemned what we would today call the most ordinary and natural pleasures:

> Do you think that man is made for no higher matters than a beast? and that you have not a more noble object for your delight than your swine or dog hath, who have the pleasure of meat, and lust, and play, and ease, and fancy, as well as you? Certainly where sensual pleasures are preferred before the higher pleasures of the soul,

> that man becomes a beast, or worse, subjecting his reason to his brutish part.

The looming trouble with pleasure of all kinds was that it could come between you and your religion. ("Flesh-pleasing is the grand idolatry of the world, and the flesh the greatest idol that ever was set up against God.") That is, if you found you liked doing anything more than you liked praying, exhorting, and reading pious books, you were in for it. So pretty much everyone was in for it, or had hope only in suspecting and resisting any natural draw.

> [Flesh-pleasing] is the very rebellion of corrupted nature; the turning of all things upside-down; the taking down God, and heaven, and reason, and destroying the use of all the creatures, and setting up flesh-pleasing instead of all, and making a brute of your god and governor. And do you ask what harm there is in this? So will your child do, when he desireth any play, or pleasure; and the sick, when they desire to please their appetite.

Many people think Paul is the original authority for this (and for all puritanism; the Puritans only epitomized the ideology), because of what he wrote about the flesh. One of the passages Baxter and other Puritans relied on most is the "fruit of the Spirit" part of Galatians 5. (I count five citations of that passage within "Directions Against the Master Sin," more than of any other part of the Bible.) At the heart of Paul's exhortation is a pair of lists: what not to do to indulge the flesh, and what the fruit of the Spirit will be.

Paul's letters contain other lists of bad things and good

things, but here the strictures have a special force. Galatians is mainly about false teachings and alienating practices, and the criteria for spiritual fruit answer the vital question of how a group of believers can *tell* whether they are going in the right way—that is, whether the Spirit is really working in them. So it is hardly an academic matter to get a better sense of the specific acts and attitudes Paul condemns and commends. Here, in the original King James translation of Galatians 5, some close derivative of which Baxter would have used, are the bad things:

> 19 Nowe the workes of the flesh are manifest, which
> are *these,* adulterie, fornication, vncleanness, lasciuious-
> nesse, 20 Idolatrie, witchcraft, hatred, variance, emula-
> tions, wrath, strife, seditions, heresies, 21 Enuyings,
> murthers, drunkennesse, reuellings, and such like: of
> the which I tell you before, as I haue also tolde you in
> time past, that they which do such things shall not
> inherite the kingdome of God.

I will go straight back over Baxter's head with my questions. Would people of Paul's time have read him as preaching against natural desires and ordinary fun? What exactly did these words mean about the way people were expected to live according to this new religion?

Picture the Galatians hearing this list read for the first time, perhaps in the house of the most well-to-do member of their church, where they usually meet to pray and eat together. They know Paul as a poor speaker and a scrawny, sickly man of the unpopular Jewish race. He may have been kind to them in person, but now they have his bad temper emerging from the papyrus of his long letter to them. He thinks his rivals should go castrate themselves (5:12), and he snarls that he is writing in BIG LETTERS for the Galatian Christians (6:11)—not that he needs to rub in his scorn: he has already called them "foolish" (a soft-pedaling translation: more precise would be "brainless"). What use might words like those in the list above have been to this church? The correct answer is not "They were another reason to throw the letter away and go back to the shrine of Isis." If we judge Paul's prose that harshly, we would have to wonder why any of his letters, not to say his churches, survived.

Okay, I'll answer my own question. All of Galatians 5 shows a great concern with the link between religion and getting along with other people, caring for them, allowing communities to thrive. Among those who had grown up as polytheists, there was nothing trite about this program. On the contrary, it set out a new way of thinking that must have been quite exciting, a hope for something beyond exploitation, materialism, and violence—a plan not for competing in purity and the denial of life, but for the sharing of life in full. The words in the list above, even the words we might at first associate with puritanical values, back this up.

"ADULTERY"* IS THE only way to translate the word *moicheia,* but here translation just doesn't communicate; it merely leaves us crouching over two thousand years of mostly inapplicable experience, including puritanism and our reactions against it. For us, the thought of religion banning adul-

*I am going to modernize the spellings throughout and make them consistent.

tery might bring up images of Hester Prynne standing on the scaffold in public, displaying her scarlet letter *A* and being harangued by her lover, the minister.

For Greeks, "adultery" was far different. A *moichos* (the root word) was a man (married or not) having sex with another man's wife, and rage and punishment were aimed at him, not her. We don't know precisely how all of the various Greek and Greek-influenced city-states treated this kind of adultery (though we are certain that it was the only kind that was illegal), but we do know well the system set up in fifth-century B.C. Athens. In Athens, adultery with a married woman, once known, automatically broke up her household, and the main victims were the children, who would now be classed as illegitimate. They could not inherit (a vital privilege, as I will show below) and were no longer citizens. Neither boys nor girls would be allowed to marry citizens, and when the boys grew up they could not take part in the all-important political life of the city along with their peers.

Since men were supposed to be far more rational and to have far more self-restraint than women, a male adulterer could presumably think through all the possible consequences, yet he chose to risk destroying the future of blameless children in order to have sex with someone in the only category—other men's wives—that was absolutely out of bounds. An adulterer was in the moral position of a pedophile today.

The crime was an especially wanton one because no man had to go to another's wife to have sex. Prostitutes were always at the ready (even for slaves to spend their allowances on), and no stigma went with hiring them, except for stigmas of taste and class that applied to the lower ranks of prostitutes—morals had nothing to do with it. Unmarried freedwomen who were not prostitutes, along with ordinary slave women by the tens of thousands, also offered chances for sanctioned sex. Prostitutes could be very cheap, while these other women—even when not coerced—were often free, or expected only small gifts or favors.

There was no romantic sympathy for adulterers, no notion of "tragic lovers," no excuse that "people do fall in love." (The story of Paris and Helen is romanticized today, but the ancients repeatedly characterized the two as monsters, who with their selfish lust destroyed great kingdoms of two continents. The tale of Lancelot and Guinevere, as we tell it, would have baffled the Greeks and Romans.) Falling in love was commonly thought to be a shameful misfortune, a kind of insanity, and decent people were not supposed to let such emotions have any influence on the course of their lives.

So it was more or less open season on adulterers. The orator Lysias, of late-fourth- and early-fifth-century Athens, wrote a speech through which a man defended himself in court against a murder charge. The sole argument was that the victim had been the lover of the accused's wife, caught in the act, so that his killing was legal:

> "We shoved open the bedroom door, and those of us who came in first saw him lying next to my wife, while those behind us saw him only when he was standing naked on the bed. Now I, gentlemen of the jury, hit him and knocked him down, pulled his hands behind his back and tied them together, and asked him how he had the gall to come into my house. He admitted that what he was doing was a crime, but he groveled and

> pleaded with me not to kill him but to make a deal for cash. But I told him, 'It's not me who's going to kill you, but the law of this city, which you have violated. You thought your fun was more important, and you chose to commit this outrage against my wife and children rather than obey the laws and behave decently.'" In this way, jurymen, the man got what the laws decree for those who do this sort of thing.

The Roman world was less harsh about adultery. A child born within a marriage was legitimate unless its mother's husband claimed that it was not—and he was unlikely to advertise himself as a cuckold in this way. But catching a wife in the act still normally meant the end of the marriage, and the treatment of adulterers was hardly less brutal. Here is what the poet Horace had to say about adultery in the late first century B.C.:

> *For those who want adulterers to stumble,*
> *It's worthwhile hearing all the ways they suffer;*
> *Their pleasure's rare, and agony infects it,*
> *And all around them savage dangers lurk.*
> *This guy dove straight down from a roof. Another*
> *Was whipped to death. A third one met a fierce gang*
> *Of bandits while he fled. One bought survival.*
> *Stable boys squirted into one. It happened*
> *That one offender's balls and randy tail*
> *Were reaped off. "That's the law," said everyone.*

This was adultery for Paul's Greco-Roman audience, and also for the ethnically diverse audience that had adopted Roman or Hellenic culture. Altogether, nearly everybody in the Roman Empire would be prone to feel that Paul, rather than making a harsh new rule, was only seconding a humane and sensible one they had always had.

BUT IS THE BAN on fornication, in contrast, such a general one that we could call Paul puritanical—as interested in controlling sexuality as his Puritan interpreters were?

If with adultery we need to get the right picture, with fornication we don't even have the right word, and there may not be one in English. "Fornication" in our passage from Galatians is a rendering of *porneia,* whose steady meaning in polytheistic literature is "prostitution" or "whoring." To get a sense of what Paul means by *porneia,* which he applies even in cases where there is no payment for sex,* we have to consider the ethical poverty of the Greek and Roman languages.

The Greeks and Romans had many terms to show disgust for a woman who had more than one sexual partner; on the other hand, a man who was erotically rapacious would not be called names, as long as he followed just a few rules, the one against adultery being the most important. Paul signaled a vast change in morals by indicating that both an unfaithful man and an unfaithful woman, with no distinction, behaved "like whores."

It is unlikely that *porneia* meant, at least to Paul's Greco-Roman readers, all consensual extramarital sex, which is our basic modern definition of "fornication."† The Greeks and Romans did not make the same distinctions about sex that we do. We think of two basic kinds: sex within and sex out-

*For example, he uses *porneia* in 1 Corinthians 5:1 for a son having sex with his father's wife.

†In fact, modern Bible translators tend to reject "fornication" in favor of—alas, still weak—terms like "immorality."

side of legal marriage. But for the polytheistic ancients, marriage was not as straightforward a matter. Slaves could not be legally married as free people were, but many had long-term unions that got some recognition, and raised their children together. Freedmen on average must have had less formal setups than the freeborn, since many of these setups started in slavery. In Latin the same slang, "tent-mate" and "shacking up" (literally, "tenting together"), could apply.

For aristocratic Romans, the nobility's separate legal history, along with large dowries, and ceremonies no one else went through, set their marriages apart. Even the Latin words for marriage, husband, and wife are not completely the same across different levels of privilege: *uxor,* for example, for "wife," applies mainly to the upper classes; *conjunx,* on the other hand, can mean a wife, fiancée, concubine, or even animal's mate, so of course it applies all over the place.

What is more, the ordinary type of Roman marriage was legally defined by consent to be married, which made getting a divorce easy for either party: a husband or wife had only to make known the wish not to be married anymore; and divorce, it appears, was common during the empire. A stricter type of marriage was available, but it was unpopular.

This, then, was the array of committed sexual unions allowed among the Greeks and Romans. In 1 Corinthians 7 (see my discussion of Christian marriage in chapter 4) Paul lays down the law for Christians and gives his rationales—partly because, I think, existing laws and customs were too loose, yet nobody in this world had thought much about them.

But across a great gulf from all of these arrangements was *porneia* (from the word meaning "buy"), which meant sex bought by the act and with no further obligation. A *pornē,* or prostitute, was normally a slave. Some had to parade naked in public places. Greek vase paintings show men beating them, evidently for fun. This was the institution behind Paul's word, and even when he isn't writing about sex for hire, he is probably emphasizing brutality. To make the word's tone clearer, here is the comic pimp Lisper (in Herodas, a Greek writer of the third century B.C.) suing someone for damages to a piece of his property:

Now for you, Myrtale.
Come, let these men all see—don't be embarrassed.
Think of them as your fathers and your brothers
That's here to judge the case. Look, gentlemen,
At how he shredded her clear up and down.
The sonofabitch has torn her nearly bare.
He dragged her, beat her silly. . . .
Maybe you want Myrtale. That's no problem.
I want my food: we'll swap the two of them.
By Zeus, you've got an urge there in your innards?
Just stuff her price in the old Lisper's hand
And bruise your goods up any way you want.

The most outrageous joke here is that the pimp in his stupidity insults the jury by comparing Myrtale to their freeborn, citizen female relatives, a species as high above her as horses above gnats.

Here is Horace recommending a cautious shopping trip for sex:

And the thigh's often softer, the leg straighter
On a prostitute in the official drapery.
What's more, she struts the wares with no disguise,

And openly displays the things she's selling.
She doesn't flaunt the handsome parts alone,
And look for ways to cover what's disgusting.
When the Who's Who buy horses, it's their habit
To cover, then inspect them: a fine body
Might rest on weak hooves. Lovely flanks, a short head
And arching neck might lure a gaping buyer.
These guys know what they're doing.

For the polytheists, the essence of *porneia* was treating another human being as a thing. If I had been one of Paul's typical early readers, whatever else I understood from his use of the word, I would have picked up that treating another human being as a thing was no longer okay.

"UNCLEANLINESS" AND "LASCIVIOUSNESS" really cannot carry a puritanical concern with purity and self-control as spiritual stunts. For one thing, the Greek words were more outward-looking than the Puritan meanings require.

For the Greeks and Romans as well as the Hebrews, "uncleanliness" was more a public and ritual state than an inward and moral one. You might be unclean, for example, if you entered a holy place without washing, but the chief thing wrong with this was that you angered divinity and marred the place for the whole community. Crime could pollute you, but this would be in a similar way. Your uncleanness was not in any important sense an inward burden—it was a visible, contagious sickness. Paul, of course, rejected ritual technicality in both Hebrew and Greco-Roman practices, and in this passage he must have meant moral uncleanliness, but the sense of practical and shared bad effects was likely still there.

"Licentiousness" is a widespread, better translation than "lasciviousness." Here the Greek word may have its usual previous meaning, irresponsibility, sexual or otherwise. "Lasciviousness" may also wrongly suggest a mere feeling, instead of certain acts. Augustine and then medieval clerics and then Puritans managed to criminalize sexual desire itself, but that was in a changing or changed world. Any Greek or Roman (or inhabitant of a Greek or Roman city) of Paul's time who set himself against his own arousal would have gone insane, because no one could escape the sexual stimulation in this social and outdoor culture: it crooned in pictures on walls and on dinnerware, in prostitutes on the street, in jokes and songs and public religious observances. (For example, the Roman spring Floralia celebration included live sex shows, and the Greeks carried through the streets the phalluses they worshipped.) There is no evidence that Paul beat his head against this culture by going further than to preach that overwhelming lust could be channeled in marriage (1 Corinthians 7:1–8). He does not suggest that either God or man can defeat the urge itself. Irresponsible follow-through has to be the idea here in Galatians.

As well as not jibing with the environment, any stress on sexual repression does not jibe with what we know of Paul himself. He was celibate and recommends it, a choice and a doctrine I will explore in chapter 4. But we simply can't squeeze out of his writings or other biographical data the inference that he had anything against sex or sexual desire per se, as opposed to the distractions and worries that marriage brought and the evil manifest in exploitative or promiscuous sex.

He had a personal torment, a "thorn in the flesh," that may or may not have been the sexual desire his calling prevented him from indulging. If so, his take on the feeling (2 Corinthians 12) was remarkably enlightened: that it kept him humble and that it was against God's will for him to ever get rid of it, but that it was a matter to be worked out between himself and God, which was good news, because God was as strong and loving as Paul was weak and put upon. In fact, every human vulnerability was purposeful and joyful in the end; he classed the thorn with other sufferings in his mission.

Let me wind up this section by dramatizing the misreading of Paul's attitude toward sex in a more graphic way than any Puritan writings allow. Karen Armstrong narrates that, as a novice nun during the early 1960s, she could not adjust to the convent, in which, for example, she needed permission to ask someone to pass her the sewing scissors during "recreation." Her supervisor at one point gave her a whip to beat herself into submission with. She obeyed, and reported back with glum honesty that the experience had merely been arousing. She was sent away with angry instructions to beat herself harder.

Would the Paul we know through his writings, and whom we can know even better against the background of Greco-Roman culture, conceivably have treated anyone this way?

"IDOLATRY," OF COURSE, means worshipping an object. As in the case of adultery, accurate translation can still leave the modern reader with no idea of Paul's focus, as opposed to what later interpreters have done with him. Baxter rants about the "flesh" as an "idol," passionately worshipped to the exclusion of God; "flesh-pleasing" is "idolatry" in that it consumes devotion.

The Hebrews and Paul had the opposite problem with

idolatry. It was somewhat like "fornication"/*porneia,* crude and shallow and transactional, but worse, because one party was self-evidently not sentient (or in the case of an animal, sentient but not intelligent), while the act was supposed to be religious, so that the transaction was fictional while alleged to be transcendent. People can worship only a living, thinking God with all their heart, soul, mind, and strength.

The Greeks and Romans may have been ripe for this. The educated among them, to whom the notion of objects' having divinity was a fairy tale, could at times barely hide their boredom and irritation with rituals (which were required for social and political conformity) to honor these objects. Epicureanism, with more followers than any other philosophy but Stoicism, argued that the gods, though they existed, had no presence or interest in objects that stood for them.

But the animistic tradition had crammed everyday life with superstitious observances: people had to propitiate doorways, stumps, and mildew, along with a lot of manufactured images; every Greek or Roman household had at least one shrine with figurines. Freeborn children wore related items as amulets for protection from evil spirits.

Outside of mythological works, polytheistic authors and their characters, faced with all of this trumpery, tend to show either dutiful reverence for tradition or skepticism—and sometimes the two in a firm, bizarre embrace. For example, Servius (late fourth century A.D.), a famous commentator on Vergil's Roman epic, the *Aeneid* (late first century B.C.), records the story of a consul needing the sacred poultry to grant him an omen before he can go to war; when they hang back from eating the grain strewn for them, he grabs them, throws them into a river, and snorts, "Let them drink, then!" Readers must have enjoyed the punch line and admired the no-nonsense consul, but the tale is in the historical legend genre, which must support the ancestral piety that is part of patriotism, so the official cannot get away with this attitude: his expedition is a disaster.

A MODERN READER might connect the word "witchcraft" to female herbalists persecuted by a paranoid church, to the Salem hysteria, or to New Age witchcraft, or Wicca. Actual sadistic cults would probably not jump into the mind.

But Paul was writing when the view of witchcraft was unequivocally grim. "Witchcraft" in Greek was *pharmakeia,* from the root that gives us "pharmacy," though medicinal drugs were not characteristic of witchcraft: *pharmakeia* can also be translated as "the art of poisoning."

Our evidence for the evil force of the word is particularly good. First, it is certain that the polytheistic cults concerned had cursing and bewitching and animal abuse among their practices; archaeologists have even found some of the instruments. (That much archaeology I know; I myself have seen a "magic wheel," for bewitching.) Moreover, the ancients knew a lot about poisons. If witches weren't the main practitioners of the science, as they were said to be, who was? It was forbidden to doctors, at least according to the Hippocratic Oath.

Someone like myself, who has lived in the new South Africa, can even affirm that violent witchcraft exists today. There, a credible press and court system confirm the reality of "muti murders": sangomas, or witch doctors, kill people, especially children, for their genitalia and other body parts, which are believed to be love and money charms. Horace wrote about two witches in such an enterprise. We have no proof that their particular sort of crime actually happened, but the point is that witchcraft had a very evil reputation, which Paul and his readers would have been aware of, but which Paul's encounters with sorcerers in Acts do not explain to the modern world:

Now Veia had no conscience that could stop her.
Groaning with the effort,
She hollowed out the earth with an iron mattock,
So they could bury the boy
With just his face exposed, the way a swimmer's
Chin floats above the water:
There he would die while staring at a meal changed
Two or three times each long day.
And once his eyeballs, fastened on the food
He couldn't touch, had rotted,
They'd cut out his marrow and his dried-up liver
For a love potion.

Love spells could have the same tone as curses, and the same motives of hatred and revenge could be behind them, given the very dim view the ancients took of infatuation. Here is the Greek poet Theocritus (third century B.C.), with the dramatic monologue of a young woman who has been carelessly seduced and cruelly abandoned and is now trying to do as much damage as possible in return:

Grim goddess {Hecate}, welcome! Come to the end with me,
And make my drugs more powerful than Circe's,
Yellow-haired Perimede's, or Medea's.
Drag the man to my house now, magic wheel!

First, barley flour melts in flames. Come, Thestylis,
Sprinkle it on—you fool, where has your mind gone?
So I'm a joke, even to dirt like you?
Sprinkle it and repeat: "The bones of Delphis!"

Daphnis has wounded me. I burn this laurel
Against him. As it catches, as it snaps,
And the ash itself is gone a second later,
So I want Delphis's body burned to nothing.
Drag the man to my house now, magic wheel. . . !

Arcadia has a weed that makes the colts
And speedy mares run frantic through the mountains.
Let me see Delphis just as frantic, coming
From the bright wrestling school into my house.
Drag the man to my house now, magic wheel!

IN THE NEXT SEGMENT of the list in Galatians 5, we are coming home to Paul, to his most passionate concerns.

Both Acts and Galatians contain accounts of Paul's conversion, and he makes several other references to it. For the rest of his life, he campaigned for others to let Jesus bring them the same kind of salvation. But what kind was it actually? Salvation from what sort of sin most of all?

He traveled to Jerusalem as a young man to study at the Temple. Quickly, he took the part of the established clergy and other officials against a new sect outrageously asserting the divinity of a vagabond, crucified criminal. He was an eager servant of the persecution, perhaps from ambition as well as the rage we read of. It was no trivial task to go as a certified agent of the high priest to purge the followers of Jesus from the Damascus synagogues.

For many of us, the center of a new moral or religious life is the image of some evil act we have done and cannot undo. In many cases, it is a cruel act. The realization that we have caused helpless suffering is a special shock, and creates an especially vivid memory.

For me, the memory is of the dog of my childhood cringing and whimpering as I beat him as hard as I could in the face with his leash. I think that for Saul the memory was of standing over a pile of outer robes, guarding them from petty thieves. The robes belonged to men who were heaving stones at Stephen (a Greek name), who had been preaching in the name of Jesus and claiming that Jews were "uncircumcised in their hearts."

There is no detailed scene of stoning in any ancient literature I know of, but sadly the practice continues in the modern world, allowing us to reconstruct the scene. It would have taken Stephen some time to die; a stone small enough to throw from a few yards away usually cannot cause much damage. There is little bleeding, mainly bruising. The victim screams, tries to get away. After a while, he shrinks down and covers his head with his arms. Impatience, pity, or self-disgust may cause someone to come up closer, raise a larger stone with both hands, and slam it straight down onto the victim—but that may mean looking into his face as he hears the approach and lifts his head. The crowd might not stop when he loses consciousness; he could still be alive.

Saul, as he was called then, saw something like this. As he went about afterward, inflicting his culture and education, his self-righteousness, his arguing, his politicking, and his networking on more Christians, he had in the back of his mind what such things had done to the body of Stephen, yet how, when the young man went down, it was to kneel and cry out words of forgiveness. It was all in the back of Saul's mind as he set off for Damascus, but if he wanted to make any peace with it, anger and ego still did not let him.

The new life he believed Jesus gave him was beyond a miracle. A miracle would have enabled him, by some unimaginable means and at some unearthly cost, to undo what had happened to Stephen. But he conceived that God, unasked, had already undone it, that through the suffering and sacrifice of God, Stephen was not dead. And this was done not only for Stephen, God's innocent, martyred servant, but also for him, Saul, God's persecutor. In Jesus, Saul met endless good and could contrast it with the evil in himself, which must have seemed quite feeble. He could hope that the good in himself would grow and the evil would wither.

He never overcame his touchiness, his fussiness, or his arrogance. It seems likely to me that the thorn in his flesh was anger rather than lust. But he kept his worst faults in bounds, sometimes with charming irony, and the knowledge of how destructive they could be was of great use to him in his work. It does not surprise me that he tended to see so much evil in controversy, rivalry, and violence, and so much good in connection and reconciliation. Nor does it surprise me that he set out to save the world Stephen got his name from, the European Roman Empire.

And did he ever have his work cut out for him there. I believe that the everyday uproar of these parts of the world was also a powerful draw: he went where he was needed most.

I am struggling to be polite about the way the Puritans, especially, looked past this, or else read the condemnation of strife as a condemnation of anybody who disagreed with them and thereby earned squelching. Increase Mather's aptly named "An Arrow Against Profane and Promiscuous Dancing" is a moving example of their attitude. In general, puritanism is linked with violence, as most recently evinced by extremist Muslim groups. People at war with their own bodies have little respect for others'.

But what is *Paul* saying? As elsewhere in his letters, here he uses together a number of words for bitter feeling and fighting. At the end of the list of fighting words, he places the word "envyings" next to "murders" (both of these are exact translations), almost as if they were on the same moral level. In part, this is wordplay: there is only one Greek letter of difference between the two rhyming words *phthonoi* and *phonoi.* But the linking of the two words also summarizes what was most horrible in Greco-Roman life, even in the relative peace and order of the Roman Empire. Things did often go from strong emotion straight to violence.

Five centuries before Paul, the tragedian Sophocles, in *Oedipus at Colonus,* had declared life worthless because of the violence that was inseparable from it.

> *Best of all is not to be born. But if you're born,*
> *By far the best thing is to take a walk*
> *Back to where you came from as soon as you can,*
> *Since when youth with its silliness passes,*
> *What blows, what sufferings, what agony will be missing?*
> *There will be envy, sedition, feuding, battles,*
> *And murders.*

Sophocles used close together three of the same words Paul does in his list: "envy," "sedition," and "murder."

Why was the violence so bad? The Greeks and Romans were, at their best, fighters (see chapter 5). The contrast with the peasant cultures of the Middle East, where menial work shaped the lives of ordinary free people, is pretty striking. Southeastern Europe was about aggression.

Hatred and revenge were not marginal or shameful for the ancient Greeks and Romans, but matters of routine and pride. A person who simply forgave an injury was held to be feeble and a coward. How could he protect his family and friends?

Not all people were comfortable with this brutal equation. Again and again, the fifth-century Greek tragedians show catastrophe coming out of it. In Euripides, the love goddess Aphrodite, is insulted that the prince Hippolytus (in the play named for him) remains a virgin and does not worship her. She makes Phaedra, the boy's stepmother, fall in love with him to the point of insanity, but since Phaedra is a chaste woman with children she wishes to protect (see the discussion of adultery on pp. 11–15), her panic when her passion becomes known will lead to both her death and his. The goddess shrugs off her use of the unoffending young woman:

And here she's groaning, driven from her senses
By passion's goads—the poor thing's perishing
In silence. Not one servant knows her sickness.
But this love I've inspired must not fail.
I will reveal it all to Theseus.
The father will kill the young man who's at war
With me, kill him with curses that Poseidon,
The ruler of the sea, has granted him:
Three times, whatever he prays for, he will get.
Phaedra will keep her honor, but will die.
And I won't give more weight to her disaster
Than to the chance to punish enemies
So that I have things just the way I want them.

When the gods themselves appeared self-centered and merciless, human beings had far fewer compunctions. The barbarism this helped create shows best in Greek and Roman historical writings. Democracy advanced quite far in Greece, and in Rome a republican government was followed by the Roman Empire, a welfare state with authoritarianism that varied over time, but with the outward structures of the Republic intact. Even in the provinces, the public took part in government. But the rule of law was always weak, and no notion of peaceful protest, loyal opposition, or constructive criticism tempered participation. When there was political rivalry, someone always ended up getting plundered, exiled, or killed, so that a movement like Epicureanism, which was interested in peace of mind, plain living, and loving friendship, advocated staying out of public life altogether.

Paul may actually have read the historian Thucydides' famous late-fifth-century B.C. account of what happened when Greek habits of thought and emotion slammed up against public crises, in this case the conflicts between Athens and Sparta and between democracy and aristocratic government in city after city during the Peloponnesian War:

> Fathers killed their own sons, and men were dragged out of the temples [where they had taken refuge] and killed beside them, and some were actually walled up in the temple of Dionysus and died there. . . .
>
> In this way uprisings began to convulse the cities, and people heard the accounts of what had happened before and went to bizarre and imaginative lengths to surpass it in creative aggression and outrageous revenge. . . .
>
> The cause of all of these things was the desire for

> political power, which came from greed and ambition and the resulting passion of those who have become involved in brutal rivalry. . . .
>
> So every form of wickedness won out in Greece because of these revolutions, and straightforwardness, which is the main ingredient in a good character, was laughed out of existence, while mutual hatred and mistrust became the rule. No promise was binding enough, no oath terrifying enough.

The Roman historian Sallust, in his *Conspiracy of Catiline,* gives a lurid account of a young aristocrat's attempt to take over the Roman state in the mid–first century B.C. Catiline began with an electoral campaign, and it may have had only the usual amount of bribery and street gang persuasion in it. But a consul, Cicero, accused him of much more, and some fiery speechifying and a single, possibly forged document led to five senators' being hauled off and executed without trial. Cicero had driven Catiline out of Rome by this time, and the crisis ended in the slaughter of Catiline and his followers by a Roman army. How much of the violence was necessary? Cicero, suspiciously, turned suppressing the conspiracy into the most renowned episode of his career, and wrote an awful, much-mocked epic poem about it. He was later exiled for his unconstitutional acts, by people who were committing far worse ones, and was finally assassinated by the goons of Mark Antony, a far fiercer political thug than himself. My point is that, though there *were* rules, and recognized rights, and due process, they fell apart all the time because of unchecked, selfish rivalries.

What did lowly people, people struggling for food, get up to in their disregarded, unrecorded affairs, when the leaders, the role models, behaved like this in spite of full publicity and constant documentation? The mind boggles.

Anyway, it is no wonder that Paul in effect decreed that Christians should build for themselves communities that were completely different, based on the qualities listed as the fruit of the Spirit, such as peace and long-suffering.

In the words referring to strife, the King James translation is off its head. For one thing, the committee worked from a version of the Greek text that favors plurals. The things they saw listed are plainly *acts,* not states of mind or emotions. The Galatians must stop clawing at one another, not merely stop *feeling* disagreeable.

The Greek word rendered as "hatred" should be "hostilities" or "feuds." The word behind "variance" meant not assorted types of dissension and dispute (which is what "variance" meant to the post-Elizabethans), but merciless competition, often military or political. The word could not refer to opinion alone or to any expression of opinion that was not pretty vicious. "Emulations": not productive contests and imitations but selfish rivalries. "Wrath": explosive shows of fury. "Strife" and "sedition" are roughly correct but not strong enough. Americans might think kindly of civil unrest or even rebellion, but in Greek literature, "strife" is likely to get people killed for a less than idealistic cause, and "sedition," a compound word, is a cynical "uprising" that "splits" the state—this is certainly no American Revolution.

The translation "heresies" here is strange. *Hairesis* (literally "taking") can mean "choice" or "sect." Paul opposed certain sectarian movements of his time, but at least in the Greco-Roman world, *hairesis* could not mean departure from the edicts that a monolithic religious authority makes about personal belief, a departure that the authority feels entitled to punish. There was no such concept, and nothing to which such a concept could be applied.

It's impossible for me to imagine that Paul had plans, or hopes, or even secret fantasies of forcibly repressing people. In his own words I can read only that he tried to persuade them not to start swinging at one another on any excuse.

"DRUNKENNESS" IS a very straightforward word to translate. Drunk is drunk. And Paul would probably have agreed with the Puritans in disapproving of drinking to the point of falling over and throwing up. But the placement of the word right next to *kōmoi* ("revellings") gives it a much different focus from that of the Puritan panic over self-denial and self-control. Paul's mention of drunkenness is about social behavior and the health of the community.

First, drinking in Greco-Roman culture needs some explaining. Wine was the ordinary beverage at meals, not water. Normally, the wine was diluted in fixed proportions, to lessen or put off drunkenness. The Greeks were probably less moderate than the Romans, as a common type of Greek evening party, the symposium ("drinking together"), never had respectable women as guests or hostesses—usually no women at all except the flute girls, who were available for sex, so that a party could easily become an orgy. Plato's dialogue the *Symposium* (set in the late fifth century B.C.), in which the drinkers send the flute girl away and drink so little that they can have a long philosophical discussion, is very probably not typical. (In fact, the company opts for moderation because they are hungover from the day before, and moderation means only that everyone will drink "as much as he wants" and not have to drink on command—the normal practice.) A fair amount of drunkenness would have *helped* with the more-ordinary symposium activities.

Among these was the *kōmos,* a word that, in the plural, is translated here in Galatians as "revellings." *Kōmos* originally meant a village festival, then it could mean carousing in general, but by Paul's time the main image was of what went on *after* the carousing. This *kōmos* was a group of men marching down the street at night, drunk, wearing garlands, carrying torches, and making loud music. The flute girls might go along as accompanists. In vase paintings, the mythical version of the scene features satyrs—part-man, part-goat creatures wholly outside civilization, with giant penises and a reputation for wild lust—and their accompanists are nymphs, their main sexual partners. Stories of human *kōmoi* are consistent with this. Here in Theocritus, a young man is visiting a young woman to convey a come-on blended with a threat:

> *"I would have come—I swear it by sweet Love—*
> *At nightfall with a couple of my friends,*
> *And Dionysus's apples in my tunic,*
> *And on my head white poplar—which is sacred*
> *To Hercules—all wound up with purple ribbons. . . .*
> *If you had let me in, you would have liked it.*
> *(Good-looking, fast—that's me among the boys.)*
> *I'd have kissed your pretty mouth and slept in peace.*
> *But if you'd shoved me out and barred the door,*
> *Torches and axes would have come against you."*

The following account from Plutarch (late first, early second century A.D.) is probably only a legend (the events would have taken place in the 730s B.C.), but it does show respectable people's attitude toward the *kōmos:*

> [Archias] could not win over the boy [Actaeon, with whom he was infatuated], so he decided to kidnap him. He gathered together many friends and servants and went on a *kōmos* against the home of Melissus [Actaeon's father] and tried to extract the youth. But the father and his people fought back, and the neighbors as well ran out and engaged the attackers in a tug-of-war, so that Actaeon was pulled apart and killed. Archias's party then made themselves scarce.

Paul was writing not about parties in general, but instead about a specific tradition that was not terribly good for men, women, or the neighborhood.

MOST PEOPLE READ "not inheriting the kingdom of God" as purely negative, and the Puritans and others have used it as a combative threat. Put your foot wrong, and out you go. But this is based on the modern idea of inheritance as a far broader yet also far less important privilege than it was in the ancient world. Most of Paul's audience would not have been inheritors, but they would have yearned to be.

Among us, most people (though they expect to inherit something from their parents) accept having to make their own way in the world. An inheritance big enough to live on is a rare thing, but this seldom matters, as independent livelihoods are quite plentiful. It was very different for the ancients: inheritance was the defining fact for secure, respectable people. This group lived in leisure off their parents' slave-run land and businesses both before and after their parents' death, and even professions (other than that of orator, which paid more in political influence than in money) were only for those able unfortunates who needed them.

It is no wonder that "inheriting" and "the kingdom of God" go together in scripture. For slaves, freedmen, laborers, soldiers, wanderers, colonists, hucksters, prostitutes (a very large profession), artists, entrepreneurs on a shoestring, and all of the others struggling through the hard facts of the Roman Empire, "inheriting" was a fantasy of salvation.

The fantasy produced a popular comic motif, that of the legacy hunter, or person who flatters and bribes the wealthy in the hope of being written into their wills. Real legacy hunters would have been rare, as substantial people nearly all married and had children who got the bulk of their estates, and the childless tended to keep their money within their families and circles of close, trusted friends anyway. The attentions of outsiders would normally have only annoyed the well-to-do. But the yearning for inheritance was so strong that quite a lot of black comedy resulted. This is the novelist Petronius, writing around 60 A.D.—he was a contemporary of Paul's and was also put to death (actually, he was forced to commit suicide) in Rome under Nero.

> In our vagabond state, we had no idea where we were, but we learned from a passing farmer that this was Croton, a very ancient city and at one time the most powerful in Italy. We studiously inquired who lived on that noble spot now, and what their main business pursuit was now that many wars had worn through their stores of wealth.

> "O strangers," the farmer said, "if you are merchants, find a different project and seek some other means of livelihood. If, however, you are sophisticated people and can lie your heads off on every occasion, you are headed straight toward profit. In this city the study of liberal arts finds no glory, oratory has no place, and probity and conscience win no praise and bring no gain. All the people you will see belong to one of two classes: they are either legacy hunters or the targets of legacy hunters. No one in this city brings up children, because anyone who has heirs ready in the family never gets an invitation to dinner. He is excluded from public entertainments and barred from society altogether. Like some skulking criminal, he hides at home. But the men who have never married and have no near relatives hold the highest offices. They alone are considered martial, brave, and clean-living.
>
> "You are approaching," he concluded, "a town with a plague. There is nothing there but corpses and the crows that feed on them."

I can't resist telling what this speech sets in motion. The footloose friends decide to masquerade as a shipwrecked plutocrat and the remains of his retinue, so that the townspeople will pamper them in hopes of legacies. It works spectacularly—one woman even hands over her two children as sexual playthings. But the "rich man" dies. Fortunately, he leaves a will that seems certain to prevent the expectant "heirs" from finding out that there is no money and taking out their rage on his surviving companions: no one, the will states, may inherit without helping to eat the corpse in public. Unfortunately, the heirs are willing to do it. I'd give a lot to know how the author got his protagonists out of *that* one, but the fragmentary novel breaks off here.

For real people, the inheritance fantasy probably wasn't founded only on greed. It was likely also a fantasy of belonging fully, which was impossible unless you had a household—the basic thing inherited, and a very arduous thing to put together on your own. The Roman poet Martial (late first, early second century B.C.), in a poem to a friend of the same name, places inheritance first among blessings; moreover, the family stronghold in the last line here is the main thing you would inherit or buy with the inheritance.

Martial, my darling friend, the following
Are things that make a life more fortunate:
Property from a will, not won by labor,
A fertile farm, and an established household.

Christianity offered anyone, no matter how poor and powerless, an alternative inheritance—another kind of home, a new way to belong. In this light, Paul's message is strongly positive: not "Obey these strictures, against human nature, or we'll kick you out of the community you were born into," but instead, "We offer you an equal share of a community, such as most of you could only dream of before. You forfeit it only if you are disorderly, through these destructive acts that are not even attractive in comparison to the life you could be leading."

No wonder Christianity grew like mad.

A PAUL FED UP with Greco-Roman culture is not at all hard to posit. Many Greeks and Romans were fed up too. What they lacked was a grasp of how things could be better. But

Paul had one, though he almost needed to reinvent Greek to express it. After the un-fruit of the Spirit comes the contrasting list:

> 22 But the fruit of the spirit is loue, joy, peace, long-
> suffering, gentlenesse, goodnesse, faith, 23 Meeknesse,
> temperance: against such there is no law.

As many Bible readers will already know, this "love" is *agapē* (a word not often used before the New Testament). It is selfless love, as opposed to the common Classical Greek words *philia,* which meant the exclusive love of one's own circle, and *erōs,* which meant erotic love. "Joy," as in the joy of prayer and spiritual fellowship in themselves, was not a polytheistic idea. "Peace," here arguably a peaceful attitude, peaceful behavior, or social harmony, had used to mean very little but the absence of war. I can deal with almost all the rest of these words even more briefly: "long-suffering," "gentleness," "goodness," "meekness," and "temperance" are not exactly stars in Greco-Roman literature, when they appear at all.

But "faith"—wow. For the Greeks it was a powerful word, *pistis;* and for the Romans, *fides,* with the same Indo-European root and the same basic meanings, was one of the five or ten most powerful in their language. *Pistis/fides* always had to do with trustworthiness or trust, but its applications among polytheists were almost opposite to those in the New Testament. Polytheistic *pistis/fides* was good backup: a guarantee or other binding commitment, often based on scary oaths (the swearer might invoke, for his own destruction in case he lied, the combined power of the earth, heaven, and the underworld); the past experience of a businessman's good faith or good credit; the long-term reliability of friends, family, associates, or fellow-citizens; or a proof or very persuasive argument. *Pistis/fides* could also be the feeling of trust evoked by any of these things. I could quote from any number of speeches of Cicero to show the word used in make-or-break and even life-or-death situations. Moralistic Roman writers of all kinds were infatuated with it: *prisca fides,* or "old-fashioned reliability," summoned up the fantasy of a time when everyone kept his word or was tied to four horses who were then whipped to run in divergent directions.

Trust or Trustworthiness, like everything else important, was a deity; but then, so was Terror. Before Christianity, neither the Greeks nor the Romans seem ever to have used the concept in what we would call a spiritual sense—that would have broken it and re-formed it forever for them, which is in fact what Christianity did. *Pistis/fides* for the polytheistic ancients came from watching their backs. Our "faith" comes from the *agapē* version of love, from putting away intent self-protection and relying on God's providence.

WHAT ABOUT THE IMPACT of the entire passage in Galatians 5? I think it was ringing, jolting, but welcome. This is particularly because of the text before and after the lists of do's and don't's.

> 13 For brethren, ye haue beene called vnto liberty;
> onely *use* not libertie for an occasion to the flesh, but by
> loue serue one another. 14 For all the Law is fulfilled in
> one word, *even* in this; Thou shalt loue thy neighbour
> as thy selfe. 15 But if yee bite and deuoure one another,
> take heed ye be not consumed one of another. 16 This
> I say then, Walke in the spirit, and ye shall not fulfill

> the lust of the flesh. 17 For the flesh lusteth against the
> Spirit, and the spirit against the flesh: and these are
> contrary the one to the other: so that yee cannot doe the
> things that yee would. 18 But if yee be led of the spirit,
> yee are not vnder the Law. . . .
>
> 24 And they that are Christs, haue crucified the
> flesh with the affections and lustes. 25 If we liue in the
> Spirit, let vs also walke in the Spirit. 26 Let vs not be
> desirous of vain glory, prouoking one another, enuying
> one another.

I've taught literature for too long, so I can't help myself. I'm going to make a list of the most obvious contrasts or opposing forces:

True liberty	↔	self-indulgence
Love, service	↔	flesh
Love, law	↔	tearing one another to pieces
Spirit	↔	flesh
Spirit	↔	compulsion or burden of the law
Christ	↔	flesh, "affections," and "lusts" (= passions and self-indulgence)
Spirit	↔	egotism, resentment

In this pattern, parallel to the lists of do's and don't's, people can either pull one another apart or pull together. What is more, Paul connects the peace of the community with the metaphysical Spirit in a way that the English does not show. *Pneuma* (from which we have "pneumatic") means both Spirit and physical breath. What is most essential for life is most free, most natural, and most shared. In the Hebrew Bible, the

Spirit *(rúach)* of God comes to the entire nation, bringing his kingdom.

Flesh, or *sarx,* on the other hand, either is just an object or it is animal life with its unthinking drives. Animals tear at one another, eat one another. Since the polytheists tended to distinguish the *sarx* sharply from the mind, it was also a good word for a dead body. A large coffin was a sarcophagus, or "flesh eater."

Paul's point is not that the body or nature is bad and the mind or spirit good. It is about two ways of using the body, the one for a life that is worth living forever, the other for a life that is as good as death in the short time before it vanishes. The passage is not an angry homily but a shout to people standing hesitant on a thirtieth-story ledge. Community is life. The failure of community is death. Paul is writing that he cannot let his followers die.

But what best expresses this urgency is the image of crucifixion. This is what Christ did to save humankind from death. And the metaphor of "crucifying" antisocial passions makes that sacrifice seem to spill over from the metaphysical realm to the natural one: believers get not only eternal life but a life of the Spirit in community that begins right now. Christ stopped at nothing in showing his love for humankind. On his example, people must stop at nothing in showing love for one another. They must eliminate, at any cost, the selfishness that divides them.

Most people have, at least in the back of their minds, the idea that crucifixion was abominable. But sheer wear dulls that impression. Some historical facts may sharpen it.

Like all torture, crucifixion in the Greco-Roman world was for those without rights. In the historical era, constitutions forbade torturing citizens. But anybody could hurt a slave: his owner, on any whim and usually with no limits; a stranger, who would at most owe the owner compensation for physical damage to the slave, as if for scratching a piece of goods; or professional interrogators, who tortured unoffending slaves routinely for crimes committed in their households, just because slaves were ubiquitous and likely to know something or other about most of what went on. Provincials of the Roman Empire, like Jesus, could also be vulnerable.

Crucifixion was the nadir of torture. It was never careless or whimsical, but was always a punishment, and a punishment for a crime that threatened the system, such as property crime in the case of the two thieves crucified with Jesus, and such as the slave revolt led by Spartacus, which ended in the crucifixion of thousands. This was the punishment for those who, like Jesus, stepped far out of line.

For maximum humiliation, and maximum edification of others, crucifixion was public. Crosses with their victims on them might stand beside roadsides or on hills. The crucified were totally naked, without loincloths. Anyone could point and comment, and Greeks and Romans, with their intense interest in the phallus, no doubt did. Was it too large (a not unknown complaint)? Not dainty and shapely (as they preferred)? Was it—grotesque!—circumcised?

The families and friends could do nothing but watch, hour after hour. The victims died when they could no longer pull their shoulders back to keep their esophagus open and breathe. They were never reprieved. At most, they got a numbing drug or something to drink, or the leg breaking (a chop that might go straight through the shinbones) to prevent them from bracing themselves upward from the foot stand and surviving longer. This was probably seldom an act of mercy, as opposed to a convenience; in Jesus' case, the officials who wanted his legs broken but found him to be already dead were wary of offending Jews, who could not have buried him on the Sabbath (John 19:31–33). "Forsaken" is the right word for the crucified.

An arrangement was made to allow Jesus burial, but this was not universal. A rotting crucified body is a prop in Petronius's black-comic farce about the widow of Ephesus. She goes down with her husband's corpse into his tomb, in showy devotion, and is starving herself to death while bewailing him. Meanwhile, nearby, a guard is assigned to keep a criminal's relatives from taking down his dead body from its cross and burying it—burial was essential for the soul's rest, the Greeks and Romans thought. Drawn to the light and noise in the tomb, the guard seduces the widow and through repeated visits neglects his duty until the relatives steal away the crucified body. This means the guard faces execution himself, but his clever new girlfriend, in the ultimate example of female depravity, donates her dead husband to hang in the criminal's place and (according to polytheistic theology) to have his grisly afterlife. "Go to hell!" is an apt rendering of the Roman curse "Get crucified!" It is about unspeakable suffering, and it is about suffering that can reach into eternity.

Paul evokes all this in the single fearsome word "crucifixion": this is how much God loves humankind. This is the sort of suffering he gave himself to for their sake. When they give themselves to him, what effort and what sacrifice is not worth expressing love toward others?

My image of Paul is never going to be the same now that I have read the passage in Greek and followed some of its words home. How did I ever accept the fairy tale of the apostle walking into communities of happy pagans, at peace with nature and their bodies, and shutting down the Maypole dances—to the dancers' mysterious glee? Instead, he sacrificed his home, his health, his peace of mind, and eventually his life for the sake of the Greeks and Romans—whom, since they are long dead, it should not be politically incorrect to call kindergartners with knives. He must have helplessly, sufferingly loved them.

CHAPTER 3: NO CLOSET, NO MONSTERS? PAUL AND HOMOSEXUALITY

Paul's longest passage on homosexuality, Romans 1:24–27, is the single most fiercely debated of his writings. The passage is obviously important, placed as it is almost at the beginning of what many scholars consider Paul's last and climactic letter, and forming as it does the heart of his most savage indictment of polytheism. And here Paul pronounces on the most divisive issue in Christianity today.

> 24 Therefore God gave them up in the lusts of their
> hearts to impurity, to the degrading of their bodies
> among themselves, 25 because they exchanged God for
> a lie and worshiped and served the creature rather than
> the Creator, who is blessed forever! Amen.
>
> 26 For this reason God gave them up to degrading
> passions. Their women exchanged natural intercourse
> for unnatural, 27 and in the same way also the men,
> giving up unnatural intercourse with women, were
> consumed with passion for one another. Men commit-

> ted shameless acts with men and received in their own persons the due penalty for their error.

There are so many ways to abuse the Bible. The most obvious is to interpret a biblical statement in isolation from others; they are definitely not all equal in rank, as the Bible itself keeps saying. When I was at the University of Kansas, the Westboro "Baptist Church" used to picket the student union, and tiny children carried signs declaring that GOD HATES FAGS. The "minister" cited the above Pauline verses as part of his authority to disrupt the funerals of AIDS victims—ignoring, of course, the vital command to love one another set down in Jewish scripture, expanded by Jesus, and stressed again and again by Paul.

But to distort the Bible's historical context is, though a much less flamboyant violation of the Bible's purposes, in the long run a more damaging one. Think how many mutually alienated and suspicious people the Westboro rants bring together in spirit every time they make the news. Here, in contrast, is John Boswell on the Romans passage, trying to explain away the seeming condemnation of acts that were "characteristic" and "natural" in Greco-Roman society—and therefore "not morally reprehensible" to Paul. I cannot see in Boswell's words any contribution to peace and clarity among Christians (let alone others), but rather to further conflict, from politically correct disingenuousness on one side and angry bafflement on the other.

> . . . the persons Paul condemns are manifestly not homosexual: what he derogates are homosexual acts committed by apparently heterosexual persons. The

> whole point of Romans I, in fact, is to stigmatize persons who have rejected their calling, gotten off the true path they were once on. It would completely undermine the thrust of the argument if the persons in question were not "naturally" inclined to the opposite sex in the same way they were "naturally" inclined to monotheism. . . .
>
> . . . It is not clear that Paul distinguished in his thoughts or writings between gay persons (in the sense of permanent sexual preference) and heterosexuals who simply engaged in periodic homosexual behavior. It is in fact unlikely that many Jews of his day recognized such a distinction, but it is quite apparent that—whether or not he was aware of their existence—Paul did not discuss gay *persons* but only homosexual acts committed by heterosexual persons.

I'm trying as hard as I can to picture Paul standing outside the assembly, like a bouncer outside a nightclub, scanning with his gaydar (keen or otherwise) for the mere metrosexuals. I'm failing.

Wouldn't the Greco-Roman literature of homosexuality provide more insight and better terms for dialogue than Boswell does? This literature is the closest representation available of what people saw around them in polytheistic imperial cities like Rome, and what they thought of it.

A first pair of eyes to look through is, of course, Paul's. For more than three hundred years before he was born, first the Greeks and then the Romans had ruled his home city of Tarsus and made it as similar to the cities of southern Europe as they could. But however much of the Greco-Roman worldview Paul might have adopted, what he heard at home and in the synagogue would not have led him to tolerate homosexuality. Jewish teaching was clear: homosexual acts were an abomination.

But another teaching mandated circumcision for all males in God's covenant. Paul put this aside; Judaism would not always hand down what Christianity would practice. Perhaps, in the matter of homosexuality, what he saw as a boy influenced him more than his tradition did. Among the female prostitutes on the streets, or in the windows or doorways of brothels, were males, on average a lot younger. At any slave auction he found himself watching, there might be attractive boys his own age (blond Scythians, red-haired Germans?) knocked down to local pimps at high prices, to the sound of jokes about how much they would have to endure during their brief careers in order to be worth it. A pious Jewish family, as Paul's probably was, would not have condoned sexual abuse of any of its slaves, but he would know from his non-Jewish friends that household slaves normally were less respected as outlets for bodily functions than were the household toilets, and that a sanctioned role of slave boys was anal sex with free adults.

Flagrant pedophiles might have pestered him and his friends on the way to and from school, offered friendship, offered tutoring, offered athletic training, offered money or gifts. But adults he trusted would have told him that even any flirting could ruin his reputation, and at worst get him officially classed as a male prostitute, with the loss of all of his civic rights. After his conversion, as he preached what Jesus meant for human society, he wasn't going to let anyone believe that it included any of this.

Readers may think I am exaggerating, that the day-to-day

culture of homosexuality could not have been so bad. They may have heard of Platonic homoerotic sublimity or festive or friendly couplings. None of the sources, objectively read, backs any of this up.

The Roman poet Martial uses "to be cut to pieces" as the ordinary term for "to be the passive partner." The Greeks and Romans thought that the active partner in homosexual intercourse used, humiliated, and physically and morally damaged the passive one. Heterosexual penetration could be harmless in the Christian community, in marriage (see chapter 4); homosexual penetration could be harmless nowhere. There were no gay households; there were in fact no gay institutions or gay culture at all, in the sense of times or places in which it was mutually safe for men to have anal sex with one another.

In fifth-century Athens (the gay paradise we hear of), one of the most common insults in comedy was "having a loose anus," meaning depraved—not just sexually, but generally. Plutarch, writing after Paul's time but about fifth-century Athens, transmits a "smear" of the teenage aristocrat Alcibiades: that when he had run away to have passive sex with an adult man, his guardians glumly considered their options:

> Antiphon wanted him denounced [*or* disinherited] publicly, but Pericles wouldn't allow that. He said, "If he's dead, we'll get the news a day sooner because of the announcement; but if he's alive, it will ensure that he's lost for the rest of his life."

Alcibiades was extremely lucky to keep his civic rights (probably thanks to the power of his family), and he even had a high-level political and military career. But his reputation as a *kinaidos,* or effeminate, passive "queer," marred his short life. Here in Petronius is a Roman *cinaedus,* and this is a much more usual version:

> A queer came in, a most vapid and washed-out individual, true son of that household. He snapped his fingers and spewed out a ditty something like this:
>
> *"Come hither, come hither, you faggots so frisky,*
> *Come running, come prancing, come skipping here briskly;*
> *Come bring your soft thighs, agile bottoms, lewd hands,*
> *You flaccid old eunuchs from Delian land!"*
>
> When he had exhausted his supply of verse, he slobbered over me with the filthiest of kisses. Next he got on top of my bed and used his full strength to strip me as I fought back. Long and hard—what he did, I mean, not him—he ground his loins over mine. Hair tonic streamed over his forehead and down through so much powder between the wrinkles of his cheeks that he looked like a rough wall flaking in a rainstorm.
>
> In my utmost grief I couldn't hold back my tears any longer. "My lady," I moaned, "is this the dessert you ordered for me?"
>
> She clapped her hands affectedly and said, "Oh, you clever man! What a chic but earthy wit you have! Do you want your admirer to *desert* you already?"
>
> To get the person to move on to my companion, I said, "Is Ascyltos the only one on vacation here?"
>
> "No indeed," said Quartilla. "Let's give Ascyltos some dessert!" At this the pansy changed steeds, and when settled on Ascyltos proceeded to wear him to

> pieces with kissing and humping. Giton stood and watched all this, laughing himself into a hernia.

The reference to the island of Delos is about castration (the god Apollo, whose birthplace was thought to be there, was a sponsor of surgery), a workable analogy: both castrated men and *cinaedi* had lost their manhood to violence, either of the knife or of anal penetration. Both kinds of men were lower than women: there was no way to be a rare "good" *cinaedus,* or an attractive one—only quite fresh boys and youths had any charm for grown-up males.* The only satisfying use of an adult passive homosexual was alleged to be oral or anal rape—the satisfaction needed to be violent, not erotic. Greek and Roman men, in public, would threaten bitter male enemies with rape.

One joke among many was that a *cinaedus* had to pay for sex: had to pay someone who was destitute but could still look down on him from the height of his own all-important virility. The satirist Juvenal, of the late first and early second centuries A.D., gives such a man a monologue.

> "So it's an easy thing, an inviting thing, to drive my respectable penis into your guts and run into yesterday's dinner? It's less wretched for a slave to plow a field than to plow his master. I guess you think you're a tender young thing, a beautiful boy worthy of serving drinks in heaven. . . .†

*The only exceptions I know of were Roman *glabri,* or "smoothies." A Roman slave might stay in sexual service as an adult but would have to wear a boy's clothes and have all his body hair plucked out regularly. Paul's contemporary Seneca writes that it is a pitiful form of oppression.

†In myth, Zeus raped the prince Ganymede but compensated him with eternal youth and a job as the gods' bartender.

> "Though you brush aside the other things and pretend, what do you think this is worth? My devotion as your retainer means that your wife's not still a virgin. . . .
>
> "I'm not going to be rewarded now, you cheat, you ingrate, for the birth of your little son and daughter? You bring them up as if they're your own, and you enjoy getting this proof of your virility in all of the newspapers. You're a father! Let the gossip chew on that. That's what I've given you. You have a father's rights, you can be someone's heir, get a whole legacy."

Paranoia about passive homosexuality was rife. Greek and Roman men led an intensely public life and believed that they could see character in nuances of clothing and gestures. Romans thought, for example, that scratching the head with one finger was a sure sign of a *cinaedus.* Juvenal depicted the doom of any actual passive homosexual's reputation as certain—to say nothing of other men it was merely easy to slander:

> What can a rich man keep secret? Though the slaves are mum, his horses, dogs, and mules, his doors, his marble columns will speak. He can shut the windows, cover every chink with hangings, lock the doors, take the lamp away, send everybody out, let nobody sleep anywhere near him. Still, before dawn, by the second cock crow, the barman down the road will know. The master will also hear the things his head cooks, his carvers, his confectioner make up. Who'd hesitate to

> invent a slanderous charge as payback for the lash? At the crossroads too, some drunk will run you down and swill the story into your cringing ear.

There was even a notion of closeted, protesting-too-much homosexuality—but only in the passive domain. In satire and epigram we see a small gallery of burly, hairy, stony-faced perverts (some of whom, like certain effeminates shown in literature, seem to have been real, not fictional persons). They can even play the role of stern, old-fashioned moralists, always ready to denounce others. Don't be fooled, their own denouncers warn us.

How could any man feel safe in his reputation for proper masculinity? I can understand the storms of preemptive verbal aggression.

The active partner had no comeback from his callous and selfish behavior. There were no derogatory names for him. Except for some restraint to avoid conflict within his actual household, he positively strutted between his wife, his girlfriends, female slaves and prostitutes, and males. Penetration, after all, signaled moral uprightness—sorry about the image. We get our word "virtue" from the Latin *virtus,* literally "manliness"; courage, honesty, and responsibility were strongly linked to physical virility in the Greek and Roman minds.

In fact, society pressured a man into sexual brutality toward other males. To keep it unmistakable that he had no sympathy with passive homosexuals, he would tout his attacks on vulnerable young males. Encolpius (Crotcher), the narrator in Petronius, who dramatizes his loathing of the *cinaedus* so memorably, is an unashamed and enthusiastic pederast (especially of a youngster he shows in the role of Lucretia, a chaste, raped heroine of legend), though he chases women too.

Amy Richlin's celebrated book *The Garden of Priapus* lays out the system of ethics that locked people into this cruel regime. The regime included the erotic oppression of women. While Paul may seem to mention lesbianism, this was such a rare or little-noticed phenomenon in the ancient world that it is likely he instead means anal penetration of women by men. That *did* happen often, but men valued it less than penetration of boys: women were made to be penetrated anyway; a real man needed to transform an at least potentially active and powerful creature into a weak and inferior one.

The Greeks and Romans even held homosexual rape to be *divinely* sanctioned. There was an idol of sexual aggression, Priapus, the scarecrow with a huge phallus who was said to rape intruders, lawfully policing gardens through sexual threat, pain, and humiliation. A collection of Priapus poems comes down to us from around the turn of the millennium.

> "Hey you, who can't keep your looting hand off the garden that's been entrusted to me: the magistrate's randy sidekick will go in and out of you until your gate's permanently wider. Two more will be waiting at your side, who've enriched themselves with a pretty pair of pricks from the public purse. They'll delve in you painfully as you lie there. Then a bawdy donkey no less well supplied with a dong will take his turn. So if a criminal has any sense, he'll watch out, since he knows how many dicks are waiting for him."

Adult passive homosexuals court the penalty, but Priapus refuses in disgust.

> "Somebody softer than goose down is coming here to steal—in his itch for punishment. Let him steal on and on. I won't see."

NO WONDER PARENTS guarded their young sons doggedly. It was, for example, normal for a family of any standing to dedicate one slave to a son's protection, especially on the otherwise unsupervised walk to and from school: this was the pedagogue, or "child leader." A pederast in Petronius gets access to a pretty boy by *becoming* his pedagogue, but only after much work in convincing the boy's parents that he is a rare model of restraint.

Since success with freeborn, citizen-class boys was rare, predators naturally turned to those with no protectors, young male slaves and prostitutes. Besides that of the pedagogue, another telling slave profession—perhaps only among the Romans—was that of the *deliciae* ("pet") or *concubinus* ("bedmate"), a slave boy whose main duty was passive anal sex with the master. The public acknowledged such a child's status, as well as his vulnerability to being retired at a young age. His retirement was not likely to be a happy one; he kept the stigma of passive sodomy, but he lost the protection of his close relationship to his master, while usually remaining bound to the same household and the other slaves with their accumulated grudges. They may have refused him, as he would have passed his "bloom," even the status of a sexual plaything.

These threats lurk under the words addressed to the nameless *concubinus* in a wedding song of the first century B.C. Roman poet Catullus. The little boy, a sort of catamite ring bearer, is forced to hand out nuts to celebrate his master the groom's new union that has made him redundant.

> Don't let there be any gaps in the bawdy Fescennine joking; and don't let the bedmate refuse nuts to the children when he hears that his master has abandoned all love for him.
>
> Give the children nuts, you lazy bedmate! You've been playing with nuts long enough; now you're a slave to this wedding procession. Let the people have their nuts, bedmate.
>
> You sneered at the women out on the farm, yesterday and today. Now the hairdresser's going to shave your face. You poor bedmate, poor thing—let the people have their nuts.
>
> They say you struggle to keep away from your smooth-skinned boys, perfumed bridegroom—but keep away. O Hymen Hymenaeus! O Hymen Hymenaeus!*
>
> We know that you've only explored things that are allowed, but the same things aren't allowed for a husband. O Hymen Hymenaeus! O Hymen Hymenaeus!

The most pathetic portraits of *deliciae,* however, are in Petronius. Two rich freedmen, one of whom admits in a self-

*The refrain invokes Hymen, the god of marriage.

humiliating drunken monologue that he himself was a *deliciae* as a child, treat their *deliciae* almost as if they were their own children, boasting of how bright and talented they are, indulging them, playing with them—which makes clear their own emasculation. The freedmen are married but have sired no children. These youngsters are *not* proper substitutes; and sympathy with them, in fact, only suggests the masters' own degradation. Here is one of the freedmen:

> Trimalchio himself was imitating the sound of a trumpet, but then he looked at his pet slave, who was called Croesus. This was a cruddy-eyed little boy with teeth covered in scum. He had a black puppy, obscenely fat, that he was wrapping in a chartreuse scarf. He also put a half-eaten hunk of bread on the couch in front of the animal and forced the poor thing to eat, making it gag and heave.
>
> This scene of thoughtful husbandry reminded Trimalchio to have Scylax, "the protector of hearth and home," brought into the room. In no time, the doorkeeper fetched an immense dog on a chain and kicked it into a sitting position beside the table. Trimalchio took some of the white bread and tossed it to the beast, remarking, "Nobody in this house loves me more."
>
> The boy was upset at such lavish praise directed toward the brute. He placed the puppy on the floor and urged it to fight. As a dog will do, Scylax filled the dining room with ear-splitting barking and lunged forward, nearly dismembering Croesus's little Pearlie. The tumult spread beyond the dogfight when a lamp on the table was tipped over, breaking all the crystal dishes and spattering some of the guests with hot oil.

> Trimalchio, however, was chiefly concerned with appearing indifferent to the destruction of his treasures. He kissed the boy and offered him a piggyback ride. The little slave did not hesitate to mount his master and slap him again and again on the shoulder blades, laughing and shrieking the whole time, "Come on, horsy, how many fingers am I holding up?"

The bridegroom Catullus celebrates has the "proper" attitude: use the kid and throw him aside when convenient. Once you have polluted him, you can catch the same pollution by getting close emotionally. This is how twisted and doubled back the ethics of homosexuality were among the Greeks and Romans. This was what Paul and his readers were seeing.

WHERE, THEN, do we get our notion of a gay idyll, especially in the Greek world? It is mainly from Plato, with his whitewash of pederasty in philosophical and religious terms. Plato's fullest treatment is in the dialogue *Phaedrus.*

A good-looking boy makes the soul of his admirer "recall" the ultimate beauty it has forgotten through mortal life. The soul begins to grow the "feathers" it needs for flight. Lower and heterosexual natures have no chance for this spiritual advancement. Desire launches them "against nature" into straight sex and fatherhood.

The homosexual lover longs to impart his own spirituality to the beloved. He has picked someone with sublime potential and works to educate and improve him. Sexual attacks on the boy are part of the process, but are naturally cut short by the loftier elements of the passion—and, it is stated briefly, by the fact that the boy and his circle take a very, very dim view of the adult's advances. This remark suggests to me either that it is actual sodomy and not lesser sex acts at stake here; or that the disapproval of sodomy covered lesser sex acts, which might lead to sodomy.

But according to Plato, as the lover persists, the boy will come to see him as a benefactor. The lover's attentions will trump regard for friends and family. The boy will desire the lover in turn and become compliant.

The lover will still make an effort at holy restraint. If the couple do not have sex, they will spend their lives in the most blessed of human relationships and have a proportional reward in the afterlife. If they do have sex, their love will still save them from Hades and put them on the road to the highest spiritual development.

It would take quite a lot of space to explain in detail how I think Plato got away with presenting this kind of fantasy as philosophy, and got away with it so well that the "cult of homosexuality" at Oxford used his dialogues as sacred texts. He had going for him, among other things, a long-dead mentor and "source" of the dialogues, Socrates, and a long exile in which to write without the usual raucous Athenian public participation in literature. But suffice it to say that what he so lovingly paints is total hokey.

The pederastic writers, the most direct heirs of Plato's literary eroticism, force us to acknowledge how far outside mainstream values he stood. The densest source of their work is a section named "The Boy Muse" in the *Greek Anthology* of epigrams. These poems extend back several hundred years from the early second century A.D., when they were collected.

Though Plato states that prepubescent boys are out of

bounds, no such scruples are visible in the generations after him. These later authors called themselves "pedophiles," lovers of children. True, several authors state that they want teenagers:

> I enjoy twelve-year-olds at the height of their beauty. But a thirteen-year-old is even more desirable. And the one passing through his fourteenth year is a sweeter blossom of the love deities. More enjoyable is the one who's barely fifteen. Sixteen is the gods' year. Seventeen is for Zeus to hanker for, not me. But if someone has a yen for older boys, he's not playing anymore but looking to get some of what he gives.

But as this poem shows, pedophiles were supposed to want only passive boys they could treat as playthings; a young age was key. And the correct target was a child's body, a completely hairless one. Poem after poem tells of disgust at the signs of sexual maturity:

> What a good goddess Revenge the latecomer is, for fear of whom we spit into the front of our tunics.* You did not see her coming behind you; you thought you would have your grudging beauty forever. Now it's destroyed. The thrice-jealous† deity has come, and your former worshippers now walk past you.

> Now you want it, when a light first growth of beard creeps under your temples, and sharp wool fixes itself

*To avert evil.
†A pun for "smoothness with hair on it."

> to your thighs. Now you say, "I like this better!" But who would claim that dry stalks are better than tassels of wheat?

The pursuer may be enraged that, whereas he prayed for the boy to return from a journey just as he was, the boy must have prayed for the stubble he now sports. A series of poems plays on this theme, but a contrasting series shows the boy ashamed of growing up and losing his "attractiveness":

> Menippus, why is it that you're covered to the ground, when before you would pull your robe clear up to your thighs? You keep your head down and don't speak to me when you run into me. I know what you're hiding from me: the hairs have come, just as I said they would.

The parallel heterosexual erotic poetry is about degraded slave-prostitutes—not courtesans, and not ordinary freedwomen. Some men felt that they could have a romance with either of the latter—single her out, get to know her, take some responsibility for her well-being; even one in a series of romantic conquests, according to the love poet Ovid, was someone to whom a man owed sexual pleasure. Hundreds of lines, whole volumes of poetry, were about individual women or personae such as Lyde and Corinna. Boys of all social classes in erotic literature got nothing like this: their poems were mostly epigrams, which half-drunken partygoers could compose and recite. It feels as if other men, and not the boys themselves, were the main audience for the poems, in a reign of gossip:

> Son of Kronos [Zeus], I swore to you that I would never announce, even to myself, what Theudis promised me.

> But my awfully disobedient soul has soared up in the air in its glee, and I can't keep this fine news in. I've got to say it—please forgive me: he did what I asked him to. Father Zeus, what's the joy in good luck if it's not known?

It is important not to assume too much about any reality behind these poems. Pornography tends to depict a world of fantasy. But the words—in a prestigious anthology and usually under authors' real names—do shock. And given what psychologists say about compulsion in pederasty, I can't imagine only a little lust vented in a lot of words.

How could what did go on have gone on for so long? Why did parents not hunt down at least the most obvious sources of danger? Virility in almost any form it chose was privileged, but how could it have been *that* privileged?

First of all, respectable free people did not, ever, countenance their sons' being seduced.* A lower-class parent who could not afford a pedagogue would try on his own to protect his good-looking son. If the boy had to work where he was vulnerable, his father would be hovering, aware of the all-day danger:

> Just now, as I was going by a garland workshop, I saw a boy weaving clusters of flowers—and I didn't pass on without a wound. I stopped and whispered to him, "For how much would you sell your wreath to me?" He

*There is one account, by the fourth-century B.C. historian Ephorus of Cyme (in Asia Minor), of ritualized homosexual kidnapping in Crete, but this has no corroboration.

> blushed redder than his buds, bent his head down, and said, "Get out of here, or my father will see." I bought some wreaths as a pretext and went off home to hang them up on the gods' statues—and prayed to get him.

But as open and as noxious as pederasty may have been, there was, in this society, hardly any way to combat it but to keep watch. For one thing, any special measures that drew attention to a boy would defeat the purpose of protecting him. Gossip was so vicious it would put the most evil construction possible on, for example, a family keeping its son at home if a would-be lover were hounding him. What had the boy done, or what was he likely to do? Much less could the parents prosecute anyone who had actually hurt him.

I have on my desk a late account (from Plutarch) of a very early alleged episode (from the 730s B.C.), part of which I cite in chapter 2 in connection to the *kōmos* (pp. 33–34): a pedophile and his gang pull a boy to pieces while trying to take him from his family and neighbors to rape him. This is one of only two stories I know of that include an official complaint (in this case, public display of the victim's corpse and a demand for justice) and open revenge (a curse accompanying the suicide of the victim's father) against an aggressor. It is easy to explain this exception. The father could act because his child no longer had a future to protect: he was dead.

The second story of striking back at pederasty is Roman, and it *really* confirms how vapid it is to assume that, because victims and their families did not want to acknowledge conflicts, there was tolerance for sodomy between citizens, or that sodomy was ever considered harmless, as opposed to being usually directed against people like slaves, whose harm didn't count.

The historian Livy (late first century B.C., early first century A.D.) gives a version of the scandal leading to the expulsion of the cult of Bacchus from Rome in 186 B.C. An orphaned youth's stepfather conspired to have him "destroyed" by anal rape in the course of initiation into the cult: the stepfather wanted to snatch up the forfeited inheritance. But the boy's benevolent courtesan-mistress pounced on the danger that he in his naïveté had never suspected, and the government protected him and purged the cult in a reign of terror. Officials could act because no one could blame the intended victim, who had obviously been duped yet had escaped.

In such an unforgiving social world, there may have been a sort of standoff, with swarms of flaunting but frustrated pederasts and of quietly dodging, discreetly protected pupils. Here are more epigrams from "The Boy Muse":

> Stop your useless work, poor pedophiles, leave off your hard efforts. You're crazed with impotent hopes. You might as well try to bail the sea onto the sandy shore, or to make a count of the drizzling particles of the Libyan desert, as to endure the desire for boys, whose arrogant beauty is sweet both to mortals and immortals. Look at me, all of you. My past toil has all been poured out for nothing on the barren beach.

> Diphilos, these haughty boys with their purple-edged clothes,* boys that we can't get hold of, are like ripe figs on stony mountain crests, food for vultures and crows.

*The uniform of upper-class Roman boys.

Slave boys must have drained off much of pederasts' sexual energy; sex, according to the pederasts, was what good-looking slave boys were for.

> A eunuch has pretty slave boys—but for what? Can he offer them unholy abuse? Truly the cunt is a dog in the manger, barking stupidly, doing no good for himself or anybody else.

But a man was not limited to his own slaves.

> If you were still uninitiated in what I'm trying to persuade you to do, you'd be right to be afraid, perhaps expecting something terrible. But since your master's bed has made you an expert, why do you begrudge someone else what you've got? Your lord calls you in when he needs you, then he goes to sleep and lets you go—he doesn't even share a word with you. But here I can spoil you. You can play as an equal, chatter in confidence, and do other things because you're asked, not because you're ordered.

An adult could exploit an abused slave child's loneliness and humiliation again and again. It may be mainly slave children who are shown in the poems on bribery; the pederasts may masquerade as the parents or teachers the children do not have, and offer treats or rewards for "good" behavior.

> Awww! Why are you downcast and in tears again, my little one? Don't torment me, but come out and say it: what do you want? You hold your open hand out to me. I'm finished! I guess you're asking for wages now.

> Where did you learn this? You're no longer content with flatcakes and sesame seeds with honey, and nuts to shoot.* Already you're thinking of profit. May the man who taught you this die, since he ruined my little boy!

But amid the shamelessness of the poems, I began to lose any sense of how they might have been grounded, even in the writers' imagination. I stopped reading them when I couldn't get one ghostly dialogue out of my mind. The boy speaking might be a slave or free, experienced or inexperienced.

> *Don't you dare say that again to me!*
> *Why's it my fault? He's the one who sent me.*
> *So you're going to say it again?*
> *I will. He tells you, "Come." So come on, don't dawdle.*
> *They're waiting.*
> *First I'll go to where they are, and then I'll get the*
> *money. I've known for a long time what comes after that.*

PAUL COULD HAVE, like generations of Greek and Roman moralistic and satirical commentators, lit into passive homosexuality, into the victims. But in Romans 1 he makes no distinction between active and passive: the whole transaction is wrong. This is crucially indicated by his use of the Greek word for "males," *arsenes,* for everybody; he does *not* use the word for "men," as the NRSV translation would have us believe. The Classical *and* New Testament word for a socially acceptable, sexually functional man is *anēr.* In traditional parlance, this could mean an active but never a passive homo-

*The ancient equivalent of marbles.

sexual. But Paul places on a par all the male participants in homosexual acts, emphasizing this in Romans 2:1 (see below) and clearly implying that they are *all* morally degraded and that they *all* become physically debilitated from the sex act with each other. Such effects were unheard of among the Greeks and Romans when it came to active homosexuals: these were thought only to draw their passive partners' moral and physical integrity into themselves.

According to all of the evidence, Paul's revolutionary message stuck. This may be in part because he told his audience a more resonant truth than that of sexual misconduct in itself. First look at what he immediately passes on to (Romans 1:28–2:1):

> 28 And since they did not see fit to acknowledge
> God, God gave them up to a debased mind and to
> things that should not be done. 29 They were filled
> with every kind of wickedness, evil, covetousness, mal-
> ice. Full of envy, murder, strife, deceit, craftiness, they
> are gossips, 30 slanderers, God-haters, insolent,
> haughty, boastful, inventors of evil, rebellious toward
> parents, 31 foolish, faithless, heartless, ruthless. 32 They
> know God's decree, that those who practice such things
> deserve to die—yet they not only do them but even
> applaud others who practice them.
> 2 Therefore you have no excuse, whoever you are,
> when you judge others; for in passing judgment on
> another you condemn yourself, because you, the judge,
> are doing the very same things.

I picture Paul, flushed and sweating in his rage as he writes that *everyone* is responsible for what pederasty has made of society: especially those who, egging one another on in an insolent, boastful clique, damage others with active sodomy and then blame them. These acts are "the very same things," no matter who is doing what to whom.

Compare the list of horrors here to the one in Galatians that I discuss in chapter 2. This list has a special relationship to the Greco-Roman version of sexual abuse:

1. wickedness, evil, malice
2. covetousness, envy
3. deceit, craftiness, inventors of evil
4. gossips, slanderers
5. insolent, haughty, boastful
6. heartless, ruthless

Some terms here are rare or even unique, in the Bible if not in all the literature of the era: "inventors of evil," "rebellious toward parents," "gossips," "slanderers," and "God-haters." I think that is because Paul was pioneering a general condemnation of pederasty in the West and needed special language to show how deeply, uniquely evil it was.

"Inventors of evil": It did not look as if God had created sodomy, but that humans had. In its Greco-Roman form it was, like the idolatry it is linked with in this passage, essentially a worship of the self and its immediate desires, with all of the stupidity and cruelty that entailed.

"Rebellious against parents": This kind of rebellion was a parent's worst nightmare, the drug epidemic of the time, apparently the biggest threat for losing control of a son and seeing him lost to decent society.

"Gossips," "slanderers": The victims suffered and the perpetrators got immunity because of crude gossip and the possibility of blackmail.

"God-haters": Those who practiced homosexuality showed a hatred of God—wait, what about *that* one? It's a shocker. The Greeks had used the same compound word passively for "hated-by-god(s)," and some biblical translators deny that Paul makes the term active. I disagree, as all of the other words in the list denote acts or traits and not judgments provoked. Where are we with the word, then?

It is probably related to words Paul uses to lead into his blasting of homosexuality:

> 18 For the wrath of God is revealed from heaven against all ungodliness and wickedness of those who by their wickedness suppress the truth.

"Wickedness" sounds either comically old-fashioned or fairly vague to modern readers. But people of Paul's time who were fluent in Greek, if they could time-travel and learn English, would translate the word as "injustice." There is nothing vague about it. It is about hurting people. Paul pairs the word with "ungodliness" (more precisely, "failure in worship"), but he repeats "wickedness." Hurting people really shows how much contempt you have for God.

In the Greco-Roman as well as the Jewish tradition, outrageous cruelty or exploitation insulted divinity, which was roused to avenge the helpless. The Greeks and Romans didn't have a thoroughly just god in their traditional pantheon to correct these imbalances in the universe; usually the Greek Zeus or the Roman Jupiter, as supreme ruler, would have to do. Sometimes the polytheists invoked an unnamed god, or a personification, Justice. Two or more deities might work together. But in any case, judgment was coming, and the arrogant and power-hungry were going to be sorry. Here is Hesiod from the seventh century B.C., the first identifiable Greek author:

This fable is for rulers—and they'll get it.
High in the clouds, a hawk grasped in his talons
A spotted nightingale, and spoke to her;
Piteously she cried, pierced by his hooked claws.
In his great arrogance, he only sneered:
"Why are you squawking, fool? I'm so much stronger.
I'll take you where I want—though you're a singer.
I'll make a meal of you, or let you go.
Opposing power's stupid. You can't win,
But only bring on shame as well as pain." . . .
Leaders, you must consider what you're doing—
Is it just? Nearby, among you, are immortals
Who note how people wear each other down
With crooked judgments—which the gods they scorn*
Will punish. Three times infinite on lush earth
Are Zeus's deathless watchmen over mortals.
Covered in mist and ranging through the land,
They keep a watch on evil acts and judgments.
And Justice is a virgin, born of Zeus,
Feared and revered by the Olympian gods.
And when some twisted person blocks her, taunts her,
Right then she sits by Kronian Zeus, her father,
And tells of unjust men's thoughts, till the people
Pay for the crimes of leaders—evil-minded

*Thoughout the passage, this word can be translated literally as "justices."

Twistings of judgments, verdicts launched askew.
Leaders, bribe eaters, look to this! Pronounce
The law straight, and forget your crooked judgments.
The evil that you plot is for yourself.

The concept did not change over the next six hundred years. Paul's Roman audience knew what justice was, if only through missing it. They would have been surprised to hear that justice applied to homosexuality, of all things. But many of them—slaves, freedmen, the poor, the young—would have understood in the next instant. Christ, the only Son of God, gave his body to save mankind. What greater contrast could there be to the tradition of using a weaker body for selfish pleasure or a power trip? Among Christians, there would have been no quibbling about what to do: no one could have imagined homosexuality's being different than it was; it would have to go. And tolerance for it did disappear from the church.

All this leads to a feeling of mountainous irony. Paul takes a bold and effective swipe at the power structure. He challenges centuries of execrable practice in seeking a more just, more loving society. And he gets called a bigot. Well, it's not a persecution that would have impressed him much.

CHAPTER 4: AN APOSTOLIC OINKER? PAUL AND WOMEN

If you polled people in public at random, you would likely find that Paul has made his overall worst impressions on modern thinkers with his statements on women. Here is George Bernard Shaw reacting:

> [Paul] tells us definitely that he finds himself quite well able to avoid the sinfulness of sex by practising celibacy; but he recognizes, rather contemptuously, that in this respect he is not as other men are, and says that they had better marry than burn, thus admitting that though marriage may lead to placing the desire to please wife or husband before the desire to please God, yet preoccupation with unsatisfied desire may be even more ungodly than preoccupation with domestic affection. This view of the case inevitably led him to insist that a wife should be rather a slave than a partner, her real function being, not to engage a man's love and loyalty, but on the contrary to release them for God by relieving the man of all preoccupation with sex just as in her capacity of housekeeper and cook she relieves his

> preoccupation with hunger by the simple expedient of satisfying his appetite. This slavery also justifies itself pragmatically by working effectively; but it has made Paul the eternal enemy of Woman.*

Shaw is referring, mainly or entirely, to Paul's teachings on marriage in 1 Corinthians 7, but that letter also contains two other controversial passages about women, 11:2–16 and 14:33–36. The three show a whole range of attitudes, so they seem to be a good basis for asking how fair our criticisms of Paul as an antifeminist are.

I have to admit I was at first horrified to be addressing this topic. I don't think that anyone who ever wrote about "the attitude toward women," in any time and place and in any mind or collection of minds, has really taken into account how complicated it has to be. Women are oppressed—no kidding. But we're oppressed mainly by the people we yearn to have sex and homes and children with, and many of these people try to stay on our good side in order to get the same things. But almost nobody has them in a peaceful state for very long, as if the human biological family had some sort of factory defect. All of the pain and the conflict between the genders seems to circle around this problem.

How was Paul supposed to deal with it? As far as we know, he was never married himself. For most of his adult life, he had no settled home. He had women friends and collaborators, married and unmarried, whom he valued, but the roles of women he saw around him in polytheistic society were so varied that, to me, it doesn't even make sense that these peo-

*Cited in *The Writing of St. Paul: A Norton Critical Edition, Annotated Text and Criticism,* ed. Wayne A. Meeks (New York: Norton, 1972).

ple were all called "women." In fact, the Romans had different ways to say simply "woman," according to the class the woman belonged to, quite apart from the words for "woman slave," "lady," "matron," and so on.

A female slave on a farm could have the worst of a cow's and an ox's lives. She might have started out as an exposed baby, picked up by a slave dealer to be raised like an animal for the most profitable purpose. He would sell her for labor as soon as she could do the simplest tasks, if she were healthy but not pretty enough to be a prostitute. Women laborers did not usually till the fields, but they hauled water, cooked over open fires, and processed rough wool during most of their time on earth. The Roman statesman Cato the Elder (later-third to mid–second century B.C.) famously wrote that a slave who wasn't sleeping should be working, but it was more true for women than for men, who got to rest in their quarters while women continued working wool far into the night by lamplight, a scene I've encountered several times in poetry.

Women slaves (raped or consenting, but with no right to rebuff the master) usually got to raise their own children, but only because this made for a better product, the *verna,* or home-born slave. But a slave mother would have been a fool to ask for time off or easier tasks in order to care for her baby, as if it weren't sturdy enough to basically raise itself, and deserved exposure.

I do not read of women slaves getting crucified, but I also do not read of owners' ever treating them more respectfully because they were women, but instead hanging them up the same as men and beating them. In fact, some scenes in poetry suggest that ladies most often took out their frustrations as women on the helpless women they owned. Women probably tended to avoid execution because they knew better than to run away: out there, they would not enjoy even the protection that property had, and their relative physical weakness would ensure a more hellish life than at home.

What did such a woman have in common with this character in Apuleius's Roman novel *The Golden Ass (The Metamorphoses)* of the mid-second century A.D.?

> And there was a woman walking along with an abundant troop of servants. I accelerated my own steps until I caught up with her. She had gold twisted around the gems she wore, and gold woven into her dress, the clear sign of a married lady. An old man, weighed down by his years, clung to her side. The moment he saw me, he said, "It's him! By Hercules, it's Lucius!" He gave me a kiss and right away murmured something in the woman's ear.
>
> "You'd better go up and greet your mother yourself," he then said to me.
>
> "I'm embarrassed," I said. "This is a lady I'm not acquainted with." Right away I was soaked through with a blush, and I stood with my head hanging.
>
> Now she turned and gazed at me. "Look at him! He knows just how to behave—you can tell what a good family he's from. He gets his modesty from that faultless mother of his. And damn it if he doesn't look exactly like her. He's tall but not too tall, slender but still juicy, and just rosy enough. He doesn't wear that blond hair of his like a sissy. His eyes are quite a light blue, but they're wide awake and glittering just like an eagle's. His whole face is like a flower. He walks nicely but doesn't mince.

> "I raised you with these hands, Lucius," she continued. "How could I not have? I'm not only your mother's relative, but we were brought up together. Both of us descend from the family of Plutarch; we suckled from the same nurse at the same time, and we grew up with a bond like sisterhood. It's only our rank that's different now, because she married a great statesman, while my marriage keeps me in private life. I'm Byrrhena! I bet the people who raised you mentioned me often—don't you remember? Don't hang back but come and accept my hospitality—it should be like your own home."

How would Paul have put together the two classes, the farm slaves and the models for Byrrhena, and everyone in between, and created a policy about "women"? And what about the ways women's roles were changing? What about the ways the Christian church itself was changing them? And what about the other people who piled on, writing fake Pauline letters and tampering with real ones, in order to have their say in these riveting questions? The reliability of the Greek text is most controversial on the topic of women.

But when I looked carefully at the passages and the Greek and Roman works that showed their context, one thing did emerge pretty clearly: Shaw's view of Paul as an oppressor could hardly be more wrong. I'll start with the shortest but most troubling passage in 1 Corinthians that discusses women (14:33–36):

> 33 (As in all the churches of the saints, 34 women
> should be silent in the churches. For they are not per-
> mitted to speak, but should be subordinate, as the law

You breathe the sun's bright privilege from your nostrils.
Raise up the flaming signal that's agreed on.
You're the sole fitting witness for us women.
In our bedrooms you stand by us as we twist
In Aphrodite's challenging endeavors.
Nobody walls you out—you oversee
With your own eye the curving of our bodies.
You alone shine within the secret crevice
Of our thighs, and singe away the downy hair.
And you assist our sneaking into storerooms,
Full as they are of grain and streaming wine.
You help—and don't go yakking to the neighbors.

But though Aristophanes may seem sympathetic, he's really not. The play is a fable about why women should stay home. True to the reputed female obsession with sex, the disguised women use their access to the *ekklēsia* to get a law passed that is bound to cause some controversy:

OLD WOMAN: By Aphrodite, I can make you do it.
Ooooh, I like snuggling up with men your age!
YOUNG MAN: I'm never going to submit, since women
Your age repel me.
OLD WOMAN: Well, by Zeus, I'm holding
Something that can compel you.
YOUNG MAN: What would that be?
OLD WOMAN: A law that says you have to come and
see me.
YOUNG MAN: Huh? Tell me what it says.
OLD WOMAN: Okay. Here goes:
"The women have decreed that if a young man
Desires a girl, he may not hammer her

Until he pounds a hag. Should he not grant
This prior pounding but pursues the young girl,
It is permitted to the crones to seize him
By the peg and maul him with impunity."

Athenians were extreme, but almost no Greeks or Romans thought women should participate in government. There was no approved public forum for *any* kind of women's self-expression, not even in the arts and religion. They had ritual functions. Some were priestesses. All citizen women took part in public ceremonies from time to time, on special occasions. They watched, or made the motions and spoke the traditional words (if any). It was not on offer to do anything else. A few women created literature, but not for reciting in public.*

The Romans were, however, much more liberal than the Greeks. Juvenal complains of women elbowing into discussions in the street.

There's a worse kind, though, sweeping through the city,
Bold enough to endure men's conversation.
She chats with generals, looks them in the eye.
Her husband's right there—all her milk's dried up.
She knows the news from all around the world,
The Seres' and the Thracians' moves, the high jinks
With the stepmom, who's in love, and which adulterer
Got sodomized.

*The exception is Corinna of Tanagra, a Greek poetaster of the late sixth and/or early fifth century B.C., whose work—including an account of two mountains having a singing contest and hurling pieces of themselves at each other—was performed publicly. She was not a role model but a "sow."

This is probably as exaggerated as most scenes in Juvenal. But the difference between Greek and Roman women's roles is interesting, especially in the case of Corinth. It was an old Greek city, but one sacked in 146 B.C. by the Romans, who then colonized it. Many Corinthians in the first century A.D. were ethnic Romans who had kept much of their culture, so if Paul found the women feistier than elsewhere in the Greek world, this would not be surprising. He may be setting limits closer to his own Greek and Diaspora Jewish norms. Bruce Winter explores this possibility in *Roman Wives, Roman Widows* and argues that the tension was worse because of the greater emancipation of Roman women in the first century A.D.

But whatever the exact standards of anyone involved here, modern readers tend to come at the passage in 1 Corinthians from the wrong angle. It would not have been remarkable that women were forbidden to speak among the Christians. It's remarkable that they were speaking in the first place. It's remarkable that they were even there, in an *ekklēsia,* perhaps for all kinds of worship and deliberation, and that their questions needed answers, if not on the spot. Paul's negativity—even his typical snapping about authority—is extremely modest against the polytheistic background.

The satirist Juvenal illustrates how bad Greco-Roman attitudes could be. It seems that he thought a woman should never express a strong opinion on anything, even in private:

Worse is the one who hits the dining couch
With praise of Vergil—his poor doomed Elissa!—*

*In the epic *Aeneid,* Dido, or Elissa, commits suicide when abandoned by her lover, the hero Aeneas, on his way to Rome.

Makes famous poets face off, putting Homer
Onto the scale, hanging him there with Vergil.
The scholar, the professor are defeated,
The lawyer, herald silenced—even women—
So thunderous is the onrush of her words.

Juvenal does not only indicate that women should knuckle under and signal this by silence in public. He displays them as cheerfully, irredeemably evil. I am a woman, so I shouldn't find any of this funny, but his women *are* funny, like a James Bond villain with a Persian cat and a shark tank, or like Inspector Dreyfus in the last Pink Panther movie, wanting to take a quick bathroom break before vaporizing the world.

Look at the rivals of the gods, the burden
Of Claudius. When his wife sensed he was sleeping,*
That imperial whore put on her hood and shrugged
Her Palatine† bed off for a mat. She set out
With a single maid and covered her black hair
With a blond wig, ticket to the steamy brothel
With its tattered curtain stretched across the entrance,
And her own reserved cell. There, billed as the "She-Wolf,"
She flaunted gilded nipples and the belly
You came from, "emperor's son," Britannicus.
She sweet-talked men, demanded money, lay there
All night, absorbing everybody's thrashings.
When the pimp—so soon!—was furloughing his own girls,
She sadly left. All she could do was close

*Claudius was emperor from 41 to 54 A.D.

†The Palatine Hill in Rome was the site of the most expensive homes and became the headquarters of the emperors. It is the source of our word "palace."

Her cell last, with her clit erect and burning.
Weary but still not satisfied, her cheeks
Smeared hideous with the lamp's smoke, she brought back
The cathouse stink to the imperial couch.

. . . .

I'm sure you understand the wrinkled nose,
The whisper between bosom buddies, Tullia
And Maura—yeah, her—as they pass the shrine.
At night, they park their litters for a piss
On Chastity's image, flood it with sustained jets,
Then hump each other where the moon can see them.
Home they go. It's your wife's pee that you step in
At dawn, in going to attend your patrons.

. . . .

Suppose I break the genre rules: my satire
Puts on a towering tragic costume, raves
Like loud-mouthed, lofty Sophocles, a new style
Beneath a Latin sky, on Italian hills.
Too mild, alas! Pontia shouts, "I did it!
I mixed the poison for my sons—you've got me.
I won't deny the crime. I want to claim it."
"You heartless viper! At a single meal—
You? Both *boys?" "Seven would have been no problem."*

THE SECOND PASSAGE I want to look at (1 Corinthians 11:2–16) is less controversial in its text but still has some knots, and it is also very offensive to modern Western ideology.

> 2 I commend you because you remember me in
> everything and maintain the traditions just as I handed
> them on to you. 3 But I want you to understand that
> Christ is the head of every man, and the husband is the

> head of his wife, and God is the head of Christ. 4 Any
> man who prays or prophesies with something on his
> head disgraces his head, 5 but any woman who prays or
> prophesies with her head unveiled disgraces her head—
> it is one and the same thing as having her head shaved.
> 6 For if a woman will not veil herself, then she should
> cut off her hair; but if it is disgraceful for a woman to
> have her hair cut off or to be shaved, she should wear a
> veil. 7 For a man ought not to have his head veiled,
> since he is the image and reflection of God; but woman
> is the reflection of man. 8 Indeed, man was not made
> from woman, but woman from man. 9 Neither was
> man created for the sake of woman, but woman for the
> sake of man. 10 For this reason a woman ought to have
> a symbol of authority on her head, because of the
> angels. 11 Nevertheless, in the Lord woman is not
> independent of man or man independent of woman. 12
> For just as woman came from man, so man comes
> through woman; but all things come from God. 13
> Judge for yourselves; is it proper for a woman to pray
> to God with her head unveiled? 14 Does not nature
> itself teach you that if a man wears long hair, it is
> degrading to him, 15 but if a woman has long hair, it
> is her glory? For her hair is given to her for a covering.
> 16 But if anyone is disposed to be contentious—we
> have no such custom, nor do the churches of God.

Some scholars would not cry to see the whole passage placed in parentheses (like 14:33–36, discussed above), and they do have certain grounds for considering these verses not genuine. First, some of the words and sentiments sound like those in letters dodgily attributed to Paul. There is also some inconsistency with another, quite securely Pauline, part of 1 Corinthians. If the husband were supposed to be the head of the wife, the long passage on marriage would be the place to write that, not here; but there (1 Corinthians 7, discussed on pp. 96ff.) we get mainly a language of stark equality. And as a whole the veils passage wouldn't exactly stand up as, say, an argument before the Supreme Court: it does not flow or persuade as well as it might—to a modern ear, anyway.

But Paul seems to be up to his usual rough art, so characteristic that it is hard—though not impossible—to imagine that this is an imitation. As elsewhere, a clunky repetition sets the theme. "Traditions" and "handed on" (11:2) are a noun and verb from the same word, literally "the hand-ons just as I have handed them on to you." We are going to be hearing about custom and authority here.

Are we ever. In the Greek, the word "head" is repeated nine times in all (seven in the NRSV's English). Authority as "headship" leads into what to do with the physical head. In Tarsus and other cities of the East, especially among Jews, the customs around veils were quite strict, but what about in Europe?

Respectable Greek and Roman women traditionally wore concealing veils in public. Marriage and widowhood were the chief things that a veil signaled. (For a Roman woman, "to get married" and "to veil oneself" were exactly the same word.) The veil held great symbolism: it reminded everyone that all freeborn women, women with families to protect them, were supposed to enter adulthood already married, and that they were supposed to stay chastely married or else chastely widowed until the end of their lives. The veil was the flag of female virtue, status, and security. In the port city of Corinth, with its batteries of prostitutes—including the sacred prostitutes of the temple of Aphrodite—the distinction between veiled and unveiled women would have been even more crucial.

But on the other hand, society was changing fast: slaves (in these more peaceful times when fewer of them were war captives) gaining more status and security in households and settling down more often with slave partners; slaves being freed; divorce proliferating; many more women entering into trades other than their most common trade of prostitution—any or all of these things could have made the veil a matter of controversy. Women not entitled to the veil may have wanted it, and women entitled to the veil may not have wanted it. Bruce Winter puts the emphasis on a new type of married, divorced, or widowed Roman woman on the scene in the first century A.D., more keen on showing off her elaborate hairstyle than on constantly wearing an old-fashioned veil.

But this passage of Paul we are considering may cover (sorry) *all* types of grown-up women. A big mistake, I think, of Winter and some other scholars is to read the Greek word that means "wife" or "woman" as signifying "wife" throughout the passage. It can mean "wife," but it is also the usual, neutral word for an adult woman. Fortunately, most biblical translators, like those of the NRSV, opt for "woman" after verse 3 and so do not leave out important contingents.

Acts and the epistles strongly suggest that unattached women were among the early churches' most active and respected members; and would Paul or his deputies have thrown out a known prostitute from a gathering, as long as she was not there on business? Paul blasts men for engaging prostitutes, but he launches no parallel outburst against the female vendors of sex. He would have known that a large number had no choice—many prostitutes were slaves. But given Paul's strict code of conduct for Christians, it is hard to imagine how an active prostitute would have fitted into the community. Perhaps the cruelty of Greco-Roman brothels spared the church the headache of the problem in its most difficult form, by giving slave prostitutes no freedom to go and worship.

At the very least, there must have been among the Christians women with pasts. Would not bareheadedness, the lack of a "symbol of authority" on their heads, have galled them? They were entitled to be there—but the norms of the time said that they had to be there in the outfits of degraded, vulnerable beings. It was against custom and perhaps even against the law for them to be veiled. At Greek religious festivals, "women's police" would circulate, making sure not only that respectable women were not flashily or revealingly dressed, but probably also that other women did not take on the exclusive, prestigious symbols of a matron or widow. In Rome also, dress was regulated in detail: for example, any married woman found to have committed adultery would lose forever the right to wear a floor-length, heavily bordered *stola* and a veil. Any woman who had ever been a prostitute was of course not allowed to wear them either.

I think Paul's rule aimed toward an outrageous equality. All Christian women were to cover their heads in church, without distinction of beauty, wealth, respectability—or of privilege so great as to allow toying with traditional appearances. The most hurtful thing about bareheaded, gorgeously coiffed wives might not have been their frivolity but rather their thoughtless flaunting of styles that meant degradation to some of their sisters—as if a suburban matron attended an inner-city mission church in hip boots, a miniskirt, and a blond wig. Perhaps the new decree made independent women of uncertain status, or even slave women, honorary wives in this setting. If the women complied—and later church tradition suggests they did—you could have looked at a congregation and not necessarily been able to tell who was an honored wife and mother and who had been forced, or maybe was still being forced, to service twenty or thirty men a day. This had never happened in any public gathering before.

This, I believe, was Paul's ingenious combination of common sense and radical defiance for dealing with a very touchy set of issues. What polytheistic literature can best add here is some context to show just how disturbing, how distracting to men and stigmatizing to women, the lack of a veil could be. This context supports the idea that Paul was being protective rather than chauvinistic. The context also helps explain why the passage doesn't flow, why it sputters with emotion, gets incoherent, changes tactics, and ends almost with a snarl. There was an awful lot at stake.

Paul does not write of "nature" (verse 14) by accident. The ancients believed that it was female hair's nature to inflame men, almost like breasts or genitals: men experienced women's hair as powerfully, inescapably erotic, in a way that makes our hair-care product commercials look like an accounting textbook.

The Roman poet Ovid made book 3 of his *Art of Love* a women's manual for seducing men. He explicitly banishes married women (picturing them in their prescribed modest clothes) from his readership and addresses himself to freedwomen on the make—streetwalkers and courtesans. He treats hairstyles first.

We like you elegant: don't let your hair go lawless:
The hands' touch makes you lovely or unlovely.
There are so many modes. Let each consult her mirror
And take time to select what most becomes her.
A plain part in the center favors a long face.
The heroine Laodamia had this style.
Round faces like a small knot just above the forehead—
Only that, and they need the ears left bare.
Like tuneful Apollo's when he takes his lyre up,
Another's hair can lie on either shoulder.
Or tie it back, like Diana's when her robe
Is hitched up, and she chases panicked creatures.
Or it might look best when loose and full of breezes—
Or else constricted and tied tightly back.
One picks a hairstyle shaped like Hermes' lyre;
One's head props folds up that resemble waves.
Could you count the acorns on a branchy oak tree,
The bees in Hybla, wild things in the Alps?
It's unthinkable to tally the arrangements.
I couldn't—every new day adds new styles.
Neglectful looks suit many. You might think it's sprawling
From yesterday, and yet it's just been done.
Art mimics chance. "That's who I love," said Hercules,
Seeing mussed Iole in her captured city.

The most famous erotic passage about hair is in Apuleius's *Golden Ass.* The novel's protagonist, Lucius, is admiring the young slave girl he is about to bed.

There she was, dressed in an elegantly belted tunic, with its bright red little belt hitched up highish—right under her breasts, in fact. Her flowerlike hands stirred a cute pot with a circular motion, and she jiggled gently through the bends of that circle and slid her arms and legs along it, while her flanks shook slowly and her mobile spine went in lovely soft waves. I stood stock-still, mesmerized in wonder at the sight—and that limb that had been lying down stood up too.

Finally I said to her, "How beautifully, how wittily, my Photis, you churn that little pot of yours along with your buttocks. Happy—beyond a doubt sublimely happy—is whoever you permit to stick his finger in there."

Then the girl—glib and satirical on all occasions—retorted, "You poor bastard, get as far from my stovelette as you can. If this petite flame of mine blasts on you just a little bit, you'll be on fire in your guts, and nobody will be able to put it out except me. I know how to season a dish deliciously and shake a bed delectably."

She was looking back at me over her shoulder and laughing. I didn't leave until I had carefully inspected her entire appearance. What can I say about the rest, given that I have always been preoccupied with hair, so that I carefully examine it in the open and enjoy the memory of it afterwards at home?

I have a fixed and solid reason for judging a woman by her hair. First, it is the highest part of the body, in an open and conspicuous position; and it meets our eyes first. And whereas the rest of the body is set off by the cheerful, blooming colors of clothing, for the head this is achieved by the glow actually born within it.

Finally, consider that most women, to show off their

> natural beauty, strip, take off every piece of clothing in their eagerness to offer their nude loveliness, confident that they will win more approval for their rosily blushing skin than for the gold color of their garments. In contrast—it's blasphemy to say this, and may there never be such grisly proof of my point—if you were to take a woman of superb beauty, sack her head of its hair and denude her face of its natural surrounding splendor, she might have descended from heaven, emerged from the sea, she might be drawn from the waves—she might be Venus herself, with the whole band of Graces in attendance, with the whole race of Cupids in her train, wearing her own divine belt and glowing with cinnamon and shedding balsam like dew: if she stepped forth bald, she wouldn't even please her own husband Vulcan. . . .
>
> But for my Photis it was not diligent but desultory decoration that imparted charm. For her rich hair was gently slackened and hung down along the neck; clingily trailing, it just lighted on the upper border of her dress—but the ends were balled up, knotted and bound at the top of her head.
>
> I couldn't bear any longer this supreme torturing pleasure, but threw myself onto her. Right at the peak, at the tippy-top of her hair, I placed a kiss of extreme honeyed sweetness.

Notice the association between bareheadedness and actual nakedness on display. This wouldn't make much sense unless both signaled sexual availability and both were thought of as automatically bringing on male desire. Notice also the play on the idea of baldness, as in Paul, but with the opposite thrust: if women, who should be objects of desire, do not have hair to look at, men will naturally reject them. Paul writes that they should either hide their beautiful hair or shave their heads—their dignity comes from making themselves something other than objects to drool over.

Romantic odes to women's hair contrasted with spoofs of male baldness, which was considered very ugly if not downright humiliating. In Petronius, the wandering antiheroes shave their heads as part of an emergency disguise—as runaway slaves who have been caught. After their old enemies detect them and reconcile with them, their baldness does not take on any Yul Brynner sexiness.

> Eumolpus, a little looser from the wine, was making up jokes about baldness and branding. Once his stiff pretension in prose was exhausted, he turned to poetry and composed a little funeral elegy for our hair:
>
> *"Your locks, your only glory, have fallen.*
> *Hard winter has stripped your verdant hair.*
> *Your naked temples are pining for shelter.*
> *The threshing floor is glittering bare.*
> *Nature, you cheat, the first charms you bestow*
> *When we're born are also the first to go."*
>
> *"You wretch, your hair once glowed more fair*
> *Than Phoebus's, or than his sibling's.*
> *But now you're stripped as smooth as bronze,*
> *Or mushrooms grown from rainy dribblings.*
> *You shun the smirking girls. You see*
> *In your hair's death a token of mortality."*

> He wanted to offer more, which probably would have been worse than what we'd heard already, but there was an interruption. One of Tryphaena's maids took Giton below deck and decked him out in a curly wig belonging to her mistress. She even produced false eyebrows from a little box and, tracing the curves where his eyebrows had been, repaired the damage to his features. All of his beauty was restored. Tryphaena recognized her own Giton, burst into tears, and gave him her first really sincere kiss since encountering him again.
>
> I was happy that the boy had returned to his original glory, but I had myself to think about. I kept hiding my face, because I knew I was mutilated to no ordinary extent. Not even Lichas saw fit to speak to me. But the same maid noticed my embarrassment and took me aside to adorn me with a wig no less splendid. In fact, I was even more handsome than before, because my new hair was bright blond.

Ovid managed to combine both themes—the beauty of hair and the comic horror of baldness—in a poem about his girlfriend's losing all of her lovely hair to an imprudent beauty treatment. If bald men were funny, bald women were funnier. What was supposed to be severely trimmed or bald on a refined woman was her pubis (see p. 79, in the quotation from *Ekklesiazousae*), as Ovid not very discreetly jokes.

> *I used to tell you, "Stop! Don't drug your hair."*
> *But you can't dye it now. There's nothing there. . . .*
> *Alas, she hardly holds her weeping in.*
> *She hides her cheeks' red pigment of chagrin.*

Her old hair on her lap, she gazes down.
Alas, that's not a place for it to crown.

Hmmm. Is there a pudendum allusion in Paul's dismissal of an unveiled woman, that she is as good as bald?* He may well be linking uncovering the head in public to treating the head like the pubis. ("You want to show it? Then why don't you show you-know-what? But then you'd better shave both.")

Even without the joke, the range of Paul's tone here—sometimes hectoring, sometimes flattering, sometimes mocking—argues against the psychological take on him that many modern readers insist on: that he is merely a repressed and bitter man, lashing out at women because he hasn't got one and can't admit to wanting one.

In fact, the variety of pressures he applies reminds me of the passages in which he claims to have "begotten" his followers, with the implication that through his advice, instructions, and example he is now raising them. Update his arguments circumstantially, and we are in twenty-first-century suburbia, with Dad: "You can't go out in public in such a skimpy outfit! You might as well be naked. You're so beautiful—I can't stand to see you exposed this way. Don't you feel embarrassed? You *are* different from boys, and that's why you're more restricted, but you're just as important in the big scheme of things. You keep arguing, but this is how this society works."

In any case, the passage on veils was nothing like a chauvinist diatribe by contemporary standards. Again, Juvenal gives useful reference points. He can say nothing about

*He wasn't above a crude joke, such as wishing that the purveyors of circumcision would go castrate themselves (Galatians 5:12).

women's appearance, especially when it is unconventional, that is not insulting:

The purple sports cloaks, oil for rubdowns, stabbing
Of the dummy—we've all seen when they're for women.
They attack it with a wooden sword and shield,
Go through the whole drill; such a shameless lady
Could blare the horn at the Floralia—*
Or does she want to be a gladiator?
How modest is this helmeted runaway
From her sex, girlfriend of violence? One thing
Makes manhood unappealing: it's no fun.
The glory, if your wife's goods go on auction:
Her sword belt, armlets, plumes, a broken left greave.
If the girl's got a taste for the arena,
She'll sell that gear in public—lucky you!
But they sweat in delicate robes, their favorite parts
Chafe in those little underwear of silk.
See her groan through prescribed thrusts, bending over
Beneath her helmet's weight, see those cork bindings:
How big and thick they're weighing on her knees!
Then laugh when she disarms to squat and pee.

. . . . . .

No woman will think anything is shameful
Or forbidden once she's wrapped her neck in green gems,
And stretched her ears out with gigantic pearls.
Nothing's more loathsome than a wealthy woman.
Ugly, absurd, the dough gobs puff her face out.
Soaked through with goop and reeking like an empress,
She glues together her poor husband's lips.

*This Roman spring festival was notoriously lewd.

They wash to meet their boyfriends. Who would bother
To look nice at home? For boyfriends they buy spikenard
And whatever else the slender Indians send us.
She takes her time, removes the outer plaster;
You can see who she is! She laves on milk,
For which she takes a retinue of asses
To the North Pole, if that's where she's been exiled.
But what needs such a queue of medications?
What's plastered with damp blobs of bread that's baked
Out of the choicest wheat? A face—or abscess?

. . . .

The slave, poor Psecas, does the hair—her own
Shredded, her clothes torn from her arms and bosom.
The bullhide whip avenges twisted hair's crimes. . . .

. . . .

They load so many layers on, they build
The head so high in such a complex framework:
Face-on, she's the Andromache of legend—
Lesser, unrecognized behind. Suppose, too,
She's not blessed with extensiveness—she's shorter
Than a little Pygmy girl who's wearing flats,
And jumps on tippy toes to get her kisses.

THE MOST IMPORTANT passage about women in the epistles is 1 Corinthians 7. At the time, practically all girls of freeborn status married, so the new rules said a great deal about how Christian women were to live. Here is the first section of chapter 7:

> 1 Now concerning the matters about which you
> wrote: "It is well for a man not to touch a woman."
> 2 But because of cases of sexual immorality, each man

> should have his own wife and each woman her own
> husband. 3 The husband should give to his wife her
> conjugal rights, and likewise the wife to her husband.
> 4 For the wife does not have authority over her own
> body, but the husband does; likewise the husband does
> not have authority over his own body, but the wife does.
> 5 Do not deprive one another except perhaps by agree-
> ment for a set time, to devote yourselves to prayer, and
> then come together again, so that Satan may not tempt
> you because of your lack of self-control. 6 This I say by
> way of concession, not of command. 7 I wish that all
> were as I myself am. But each has a particular gift from
> God, one having one kind and another a different kind.
>
> 8 To the unmarried and the widows I say that it is
> well for them to remain unmarried as I am. 9 But if
> they are not practising self-control, they should marry.
> For it is better to marry than to be aflame with passion.

Like Shaw, most modern Westerners tend to take Paul, with his preference for celibacy, as grim and negative, urging people to give up the greatest human joys for a chilly, lonely religious life. This mistake comes partly from an assumption that erotic, mutually nurturing marriage was a ready option for Paul's followers, when actually he was calling them away from either the tyranny of traditional arranged unions or the cruelty of sexual exploitation, or (in the case of married men exploiting the double standard) both.

The language of equality here in 1 Corinthians absolutely does not fit a Shavian reading; it in fact rebels against the unmitigated chauvinistic attitudes Paul would have found in Greco-Roman households, both in his boyhood Tarsus and anywhere he traveled in the Roman Empire later.

For example, in the Greek of the first sentence of this passage, he plays down male-female differences. He does not actually write, "It is well for a *man* not to touch a woman," but "It is well for a *person* not to touch a woman." As I've mentioned before, an *anēr* is someone anatomically male, and with all of the male qualities of mind and morals that the polytheists revered. But an *anthrōpos* (Paul's word) is just a human being. The male deciding whether or not to have sex is not a brave and noble phallus on legs, who, if he is a Greek or Roman, has broad sexual entitlements. He is a person, a word that can apply to women too.

"The unmarried" are not only women; the word is grammatically masculine plural, but it refers to men and women both. (It is like the English word "actors" used for everyone in the profession, male and female. There has to be a special reason to specify "actresses.") The word "widows," too, may be wrong: the masculine form of the word (different by only a single letter) has some manuscript-based claim to belonging in the text here instead, and it means "widows and widowers."

This kind of evenhandedness could result only from a huge wrench away from the past. Paul, in the polytheistic world, was not only putting brand-new limits on male desire but licensing female desire, which had been under a regime of zero tolerance.

The reason the Greeks and Romans took so little trouble to control men is that, in their eyes, men were naturally sane and civilized. Women, on the other hand—this was the folk wisdom that helped shape all of those sociopathic female characters in literature—were by nature wild, lustful, and depraved. Their families had to keep them under guard and make all of their major choices for them; their husbands had to keep them pregnant; and the whole society had to stifle their individuality and self-expression, because any thought or energy at their own disposal was likely to create lewd adventures, leading to chaos and violence.

Ovid in the *Art of Love* gives a goofy version of women's character, but he had the full authority of his culture behind him.

Desire in us is saner and more sparing.
A man on fire observes the bounds of law.
What about Byblis, whose forbidden passion
For her brother made her bravely hang herself?
Myrrha loved her father as no daughter should,
And now she's bound in bark and hidden away.
The tears she pours down from that fragrant tree
Are an ointment that commemorates her name.
On Ida's forest-shaded heights, There happened
To live a white bull, the glory of the herd,
With a slight mark of black between his horns—
The single stain on all his milky body.
All of the Gnosian and Cydonian heifers
Thought that he'd make a nice weight on their backs.
Pasiphaë was his very eager girlfriend,*
Who looked on pretty cows with jealous hatred.
Everyone knows it happened! Even Cretans,
Those famous liars in their hundred cities,
Admit it! And I hear she plucked fresh leaves

*The queen of Crete, consort of King Minos, fell in love with a bull. In a cow suit made by Daedalus, she consummated her passion and gave birth to the Minotaur ("Bull of Minos"), a human with a bull's head who was to live in the labyrinth beneath the palace and devour prisoners sent as tribute.

And tender grass for him, a brand new hobby.
She joined the herd herself, without a thought
For her husband; she preferred a bull to Minos.
Pasiphaë, why those expensive dresses?
Your boyfriend's got no eye for stuff like that.
You're off to the mountain herds, and take a mirror.
You try so many hairstyles, like a fool.
Your mirror says you're not a cow. Believe it!
What you really, really want's a pair of horns.
If Minos is okay, don't cheat on him.
If you've got to cheat, then do it with a man!
They say the queen would leave her royal bedroom
*For the wooded mountains, like a raving Bacchant.**
Often she gave a cow a look to kill,
And asked, "What does my master see in her?
Look at her prancing for him on the young grass!
I bet she thinks she's pretty—idiot!"—
Then ordered them to take the innocent creature
From the herd and drag her under the curved plow;
Or gave her as a phony sacrifice,
And gleefully held up her rival's entrails.
Often she offered up the competition,
Taunting their guts: "See how he likes you now!"
She wanted to be Io or Europa,†
One bovine, and one riding on a bovine.
Fooled by the wooden heifer, the herd's leader

*An ecstatic follower of the wine god Bacchus or Dionysus (see pp. 173–74).

†Two women of mythology, the first of whom was transformed into a cow by Jupiter to hide her from his wife Juno, the second kidnapped by him in the form of a tame bull: she climbed onto his back, and he swam across the sea with her.

Knocked her up. You could tell who was the father
From the baby.

Since women were supposed to stop at nothing once they got started, Greek and Roman husbands had the opposite notion to that of Victorian husbands as to why they could be sexually selfish: it wasn't that women, or good women, were not responsive; it was that any woman was all too responsive. If you indulged your wife, you nursed a monster. You must marry a very young, very sheltered girl and make sure that she never took it into her head that she was there for anything besides childbearing. The poet Lucretius (mid–first century B.C.), for example, warns husbands against letting their wives move their hips during sex, which was supposed to send the semen off course.

Paul's Jewish tradition put some equal sexual duties and restrictions on husbands and wives, but there also the aim was pregnancy: a couple had to have sex around the time the wife ovulated, and must not have sex when she could not conceive. Paul comes up with something altogether new: husbands and wives must have sex with each other on demand, because they both need it—it's the reason they got married. According to these verses, they may need it equally. The rules for marriage treat human sexuality as a part of nature that needs expression.

History or, if you like, providence may have worked rather ironically to our benefit. Paul's main concern was to make room for celibacy, which could give his followers more freedom and a closer relationship with God; and he also sought communal order and rationality in this time of change and excitement. But nevertheless his new rules give the proper basis for marriage, the erotic one; and they also address the chief reasons that marriages break down: the failure of partners to act generously toward each other, keeping intimacy after any passion is gone; and the loss of trust, typical when men have greater freedom and a smaller stake in the relationship.

The supreme serendipity is that, in founding communities that could shelter the celibate, Paul changed people's experience of their emotions and their bodies in ways that inevitably changed marriage, though the new kind did not send down deep roots until the modern age and the end of the authoritarianism that began to blight the church in the generations after Paul. But real marriage is as secure a part of the Christian charter, and as different from anything before or since, as the command to turn the other cheek.

Greco-Roman literature gives an idea of the questions Christians may have been asking about this choice now in their own hands: faithful marriage or celibacy.

First of all, where were the parents? Parents married off their children, by right. I don't know any factual pre-Christian case of a child's defiance, which would have led to public outrage, disinheritance, or even death.*

Greek New Comedy and Roman comedy show the kind of fantasies people had when they could not choose their own spouses. But since the stories are set in the real, everyday Greco-Roman world, the fictional happy ending for the young couple in love can come about only through absurd

*Since most girls first married at around fourteen, and men as late as their early thirties, many men would find themselves free to choose their spouses, but only because their fathers were dead before the occasion arose. Even then, they seem never to have made choices that would have appalled their fathers but to have married within their own classes and on a sound business footing. Their duties to their clans did not change.

coincidences: for example, the girl is a slave just about to start in prostitution (so she is a virgin the young man can actually meet), but she is also his heiress cousin, kidnapped as a baby by pirates and now miraculously restored to her parents through the recognition of talismans she has somehow managed to keep (so that her prospective father-in-law can opt for the marriage from the usual motives).

Parental authority weighs on the legend of Acontius and Cydippe, in the third-century B.C. Alexandrian poet Callimachus and in Ovid. At a religious festival, the young man Acontius connives to secure the girl he has glimpsed and fallen in love with, Cydippe, by tossing her an apple with the inscription *"I swear by Artemis to marry Acontius"* to innocently read aloud. (He can, of course, not decently speak to her, and he must move fast before she reenters the seclusion of her home.) Though terrible consequences will follow if she breaks the oath, neither party dares to tell what has happened. Cydippe three times sickens almost to death when her parents prepare for her marriage to another man, but her father learns the truth only by a visit to an oracle; she confirms the story when he returns home.

When Christianity gave girls and young men a rationale for refusing to marry at all, chaos apparently broke loose. Girls are said to have been jailed but persistent; tortured and mutilated but restored to wholeness; sold into prostitution but converting their would-be clients or turned to impenetrable rock; marrying but managing to persuade the groom on the wedding night not to have sex but to become a partner in chastity. They stayed virgins literally by miracles.

Unconvincing as many of the tales are, they point up hard facts: respectable Greeks and Romans were expected to marry; parents were the enforcers, backed up by state authority. Celibacy was a rare and very specific religious privilege, peopling such small institutions as the College of Vestal Virgins in Rome. Celibacy by free choice seemed to mean that the generations could stop at the whim of inexperienced young people.

Another question for newcomers to Christianity would be where the patriarchal husband had gone. Families kept legal ties to the daughters they married off, but this only prevented utter dependence, when men approaching what passed for middle age married pubescent girls. There is a Greek version of such a marriage in Xenophon (fourth century B.C.). A husband proudly tells a friend how he trained his new bride, starting with a question he himself answered at quite tedious length: "Tell me, wife, have you realized the rationale on which I took you and your parents gave you to me?"

Here, in a wedding song of Catullus, is a more dramatic, Roman version of a couple with the same kind of age difference. The poet addresses the evening star that signals the time of consummation:

> *Hesperus, what sky-crossing fire is crueler?*
> *You tear the daughter from her mother's arms.*
> *She clings—yet you still tear her from her mother*
> *And give the chaste girl to the burning young man.*
> *Are enemies in a captured city crueler? . . .*
>
> *Virgin, you must not fight with such a husband.*
> *It isn't right—your father gave you to him,*
> *Your* father, *and your mother—you must mind them.*
> *They own a part of your virginity:*
> *Your father's granted a third, your mother a third.*

Only a third is yours: you are outvoted.
They gave their rights to their son-in-law with the dowry.

By what miracle could the women in Paul's churches be expected to exercise any equal authority in marriage, let alone over the quintessentially male domain of sex? Faithfulness now applied equally to both men and women—a real shocker.

It would be hard to say which literary passage best dramatizes how complete a Greek or Roman male's right to adultery was (as long as he left other men's wives and virgin daughters alone). It would be like trying to find one passage in modern European literature that, better than all others, illustrates the belief in the right to bodily integrity. The ancient belief in men's right to range is just as implicit in the entire way they lived and in a great many of the stories they told. I have read of considerate men staying faithful to their wives within the walls of home, keeping their hands off the slaves (male and female) and not bringing women (or little boys) home; and some authors felt that this was the only decent way to behave. But I have never seen any hint that a wife was entitled to challenge what her husband did outside: any speculating or accusing was nagging. Juvenal shows wives selfishly, viciously keeping their husbands awake with their jealousy.

But what about a passage showing the utter lack of male embarrassment about roaming? This one is from Homer's *Iliad,* an oral epic written down in the eighth century B.C. Hera, the queen of the gods, has had a makeover by Aphrodite, the goddess of love. She is plotting to seduce her consort Zeus away from his lookout onto the Trojan battlefield, so that the warriors she champions in opposition to him can have a chance. She rivets his attention just as she has planned, and this is how he gives voice to his desire for her.

> *"Right now let's have a good time making love.*
> *No goddess and no woman, until now,*
> *Has overwhelmed my heart so powerfully:*
> *Not Ixion's wife, my lover, who gave birth*
> *To Perithous, a counselor like us gods;*
> *Not Acrisius's daughter Danaë, with trim ankles,*
> *Who gave me Perseus, the world's greatest warrior;*
> *And not the child of famous Phoenix—Minos*
> *And godlike Rhadamanthus came from her;*
> *Or Semele and Alcmene—both in Thebes:*
> *Semele, who blessed mortals with Dionysus;*
> *Alcmene, mother of brave Heracles;*
> *Or the queen Demeter with her lovely hair;*
> *Or splendid Leto, no—and not yourself:*
> *Such sweet desire for you has seized me now."*

The speech is an epic poet's joke. The king of the gods, unlike lowly mankind, can have sex with married women, deflower respectable virgins, acknowledge his illegitimate children, and burble about it all to his wife—just as, in our storytelling tradition, James Bond can have erotic adventures with superhuman ease. But to get a sense of the difference in background values, try to imagine James Bond married and making this speech to his wife. Would he still be the good guy?

Paul does not care how unquestioned men's freedoms were. The word *porneia,* or "sexual immorality" (see my discussion in chapter 2), seems not only to forbid any sex outside of marriage (not necessarily a legal union, but a permanent and responsible one) for *either* partner, but also to label such an act with loathing.

Paul lays down the law of equality with these common business terms, stressing mutually binding rules:

opheilē: "conjugal rights": normally a "debt" of money
exousia: "authority," including state authority (see pp. 142–43 for both of these words)
aposterō: "deprive": normally "defraud," "refuse payment," "default"

It was now going to matter whether spouses filled each other's needs: this was the new law and ethic for them. This, again, contrasts wildly with rules for marriage among the polytheists. *Against Neaira* is the prosecution's speech in a late-fourth- or early-fifth-century B.C. revenge lawsuit against a man for allegedly marrying a former courtesan and marrying off her daughter to an Athenian religious official, so that she would be making sacrifices on the city's behalf. That is, the plaintiff, as he is entitled to do, seeks to ruin a man for taking a woman he loved out of prostitution and trying to provide for her child.

Julius Caesar's wife Pompeia was hosting an all-female night ritual that a notorious playboy allegedly invaded in disguise. Caesar was not interested in whether his wife was actually at fault or tainted, but divorced her by messenger, perhaps the next morning. His famous explanation for why he had acted without any proof was that he thought his wife should not even be under suspicion.

Paul's idea for how a marriage should work was the fulfillment of the Jewish scriptural command that a married couple was to be "one flesh" (Genesis 2:24, echoed by Jesus in

Matthew 19:5–6 and Mark 10:7–8). The husband should treat the wife's body as his own and serve its most intimate needs, and vice versa. The only higher obligations are to God; the couple should approach even these only in collaboration with each other: that is how important peace and equality in a marriage are. Where, if not from a brain fever, did Shaw pick up the idea of a Pauline wife as a sexual and domestic servant?

> 10 To the married I give this command—not I but
> the Lord—that the wife should not separate from her
> husband 11 (but if she does separate, let her remain
> unmarried or else be reconciled to her husband), and
> that the husband should not divorce his wife.
>
> 12 To the rest I say—I and not the Lord—that if any
> believer has a wife who is an unbeliever, and she con-
> sents to live with him, he should not divorce her. 13
> And if any woman has a husband who is an unbeliever,
> and he consents to live with her, she should not divorce
> him. 14 For the unbelieving husband is made holy
> through his wife, and the unbelieving wife is made
> holy through her husband. Otherwise, your children
> would be unclean, but as it is, they are holy. 15 But if
> the unbelieving partner separates, let it be so; in such
> a case the brother or sister is not bound. It is to peace
> that God has called you. 16 Wife, for all you know, you
> might save your husband. Husband, for all you know,
> you might save your wife.

Here was another urgent question for the Corinthians. Is this *it* about children? Only that the religious differences of their parents do not taint them? Traditionally, legitimate children were what marriage was *for.* It certainly wasn't for channeling a man's sexual energy—which could go nearly anywhere—and the whole of a woman's energy belonged to her household, to her children most of all.

Some people might feel that the ancient emphasis on fertility and child rearing in marriage had a lot going for it, but the reality looks rather joyless, with both husbands and wives—especially wives—locked into biological production, like farm animals. And getting the *right* products—sturdy, flawlessly formed boys—was so important that infant exposure, especially of girls, was routine. The law forbidding the Romans to let a deformed newborn of either sex live was in the Twelve Tables, which had a status somewhat like that of the U.S. Constitution today. Child-centered this system wasn't.

A Roman wife and mother of the highest status is not someone I envy. She came second to both her husband's parents and her own children. This could, of course, be a problem in a pinch. In Vergil's story of a divinely led escape from the sack of Troy that starts the hero Aeneas on the journey to the founding of Rome, the wife literally comes last. Aeneas is narrating:

> *"My father rose up, conquered by the truth.*
> *In reverence for that sacred star he prayed:*
> *'No more delay! Gods of my fathers, lead me:*
> *I'll follow. Save my family, save my grandson.*
> *This was your sign, and Troy is in your power—*
> *So I will yield and go with you, my son.'*
> *Now through the walls the fire's roar grew louder.*
> *The blasts of heat were rolling closer to us.*
> *'Dear father, let them set you on my shoulders.*

I'll carry you—you will not weigh me down.
Whatever happens, it will be one peril
Or rescue for us both. Our little Iulus
Will walk with me. My wife will follow, far back. . . .'
And now I pulled a tawny lion skin
Over my bending neck and brawny shoulders
And took my load. My little Iulus's fingers
Were twined in mine; he trotted by my long steps.
Behind me came my wife. We went our dark way.
Before I hadn't minded the Greeks' spears
Hurled at me, or the Greeks in crowds, attacking.
Now every gust and rustle panicked me
Because of whom I led and whom I carried.
Now I approached the gates. The journey seemed
Finished, when suddenly a massive tramping
Sounded. My father, spying through the shadows,
Shouted, 'Run—run, my boy! They're coming close!
I see shields flashing, and the glint of bronze.'
Some enemy god then seized me in my terror
And stole my reason. Byways led me running
Beyond the streets of the familiar city.
And there, my wife, Creusa—no!—was stolen
By fate, or strayed, or else collapsed, exhausted.
Who knows? We never saw her anymore.
I did not think of her or note her absence
Before we reached the mound and ancient shrine
Of Ceres."

Aeneas is commendably if tardily upset at the thought of what might happen to her, alone in a city that an army with ten years of siege frustration is sacking. He returns to seek her, and just the right turn of melodrama follows. She is dead and out of the way of Aeneas's future dynasty, but her ghost is self-effacing enough to allow her widower a full howl over his lost treasure:

> *"I went on, in my race to search the buildings,*
> *But the poor apparition of Creusa*
> *Came to me, taller than the living woman.*
> *Shock choked my voice and stood my hair on end,*
> *But what she said was soothing to my soul:*
> *'Why do you rave and revel in this sorrow,*
> *Sweet husband? It was by the will of heaven*
> *This came about. It is not right to take me.*
> *The king of high Olympus will not let you.*
> *In your long exile you will plow a wide sea*
> *Clear to the West, where Tiber's Lydian water*
> *Sweeps smoothly through rich fields of warriors.*
> *A prosperous kingdom and a royal wife*
> *Are yours. So weep no longer, though you love me.*
> *I am a Trojan—Venus is your mother:*
> *I will not serve Greek mothers in the cities*
> *Of arrogant Myrmidons and Dolopians.*
> *The gods' great mother keeps me on these shores.*
> *Farewell. Cherish the child that we created.' "*

Cato the Younger, a paragon of Roman rectitude in the mid–first century B.C., gave his wife away to a friend for childbearing once she had borne him as many children as he wanted. The poet Lucan, a contemporary of Paul, shows her dashing back to Cato fresh from the funeral of her second husband and demanding to marry him again so that—now that she is no longer fertile—she can at least share the hardships brought by the invasion that is beginning.

As far as Romans of the first century A.D. were going beyond these traditional ideas about the purpose of marriage, we read that they were going shallow, not deep, with decisions made on the basis of convenience, physical beauty, or money—whimsical divorces, reckless adultery, and routine abortions. Juvenal reacts in his usual melodramatic way:

It's tough to board ship on a husband's orders.
The bilge reeks, and the heavens spin above.
A wife barfs on her husband. For her boyfriend,
She's iron-gutted, lunches with the sailors,
Strolls on the stern, and plays with gnarly ropes. . . .

. . . .

"Why does Censennia's husband say she's splendid?"
She brought a million, so he calls her chaste.
Yes, he's aflame—her dowry shoots Love's arrows.
A man's greed lets his wife, free as a widow,
Gesture or write to her lovers while he's there.
"But why's Sertorius hot for Bibula?"
Shake out the truth: he loves his wife's face only.
Three wrinkles, and some dryness, and some sagging,
And darker teeth, and eyes a little squinty—
He's free: "Go pack your bags. Get out of here.
You just annoy me now. You keep on snuffling.
Get out—fast. I'll replace you with a dry nose. . . ."

. . . .

But now she abdicates,
Changes her home, wears out her bridal veil,
Then flees back to the still-squashed bed she scorned,
Leaving the wedding's decorated awnings,
And the greenery not yet withered on the door. . . .

. . . .

The Phrygian sage, the rented Indian
Skilled in astrology advise the rich.
For the poor, the rampart and the circus settle
Destiny. The bare neck with its long gold chain
Asks at the pillars and the dolphin column
Whether to dump the barkeep for the ragman.

Poor women bear the dangers, though, of childbirth
And all the work of nursing—fate compels them.
New mothers seldom lie in gilded beds.
That's what the expertise in drugs achieves.

A marriage—or a divorce—for spiritual purposes was unheard of up until Christianity, and was entirely against Greco-Roman social norms. Paul's vocabulary itself moves toward change. In verses 10 and 11 are the traditional terms, pointing to the spiritually poisonous traditional gap in power: the wife must not "separate" from her husband—or if she does, she must either stay unmarried or become reconciled to the same man—and the husband must not "divorce" his wife (literally "throw out," the same word as for disowning a child). Under the laws of the Greeks and Romans, the wife could only remove herself, forfeiting her home and children; the husband, in a divorce, sent the wife back to her parents' house with nothing but her dowry, and if she had neither parents nor a dowry, he could put her on the street. Nothing could entitle her to a share in his home or to a new one of her own.

But in the following sentences, Paul uses "divorce" for both husbands and wives. When it comes to religion, Christian women as well as Christian men can in extreme circumstances "throw out" their spouses. Paul wants the couple to stay married, but if the unbeliever chooses otherwise, the believer, male or female, "is not bound," which literally means "is not a slave." Again, I just don't see where Shaw and his fellow critics get off.

> 25 Now concerning virgins, I have no command of the Lord, but I give my opinion as one who by the Lord's mercy is trustworthy. 26 I think that, in view of the impending crisis, it is well for you to remain as you are. 27 Are you bound to a wife? Do not seek to be free. Are you free from a wife? Do not seek a wife. 28 But if you marry, you do not sin, and if a virgin marries, she does not sin. Yet those who marry will experience distress in this life, and I would spare you that. 29 I mean, brothers and sisters, the appointed time has grown short; from now on, let even those who have wives be as though they had none, 30 and those who mourn as though they were not mourning, and those who rejoice as though they were not rejoicing, and those who buy as though they had no possessions, 31 and those who deal with the world as though they had no dealings with it. For the present form of this world is passing away.
>
> 32 I want you to be free from anxieties. The unmarried man is anxious about the affairs of the Lord, how to please the Lord; 33 but the married man is anxious about the affairs of the world, how to please his wife, 34 and his interests are divided. And the unmarried woman and the virgin are anxious about the affairs of the Lord, so that they may be holy in body and spirit; but the married woman is anxious about the affairs of the world, how to please her husband. 35 I say this for

> your own benefit, not to put any restraint upon you,
> but to promote good order and unhindered devotion to
> the Lord.
>
> 36 If anyone thinks that he is not behaving properly
> towards his fiancée, if his passions are strong, and so it
> has to be, let him marry as he wishes; it is no sin. Let
> them marry. 37 But if someone stands firm in his
> resolve, being under no necessity but having his own
> desire under control, and has determined in his own
> mind to keep her as his fiancée, he will do well. 38 So
> then, he who marries his fiancée does well; and he who
> refrains from marriage will do better.
>
> 39 A wife is bound as long as her husband lives. But
> if the husband dies, she is free to marry anyone she
> wishes, only in the Lord. 40 But in my judgment she
> is more blessed if she remains as she is. And I think
> that I too have the Spirit of God.

That word "blessed/happy" is the crescendo of the discussion of marriage. For the Greeks, this word had specifically meant the following:

1. divine
2. divinely favored
3. lucky
4. rich
5. dead

To Greek and Roman readers, Paul might have seemed to be making a strange connection here, in this final part of the passage, between Epicurean ideas of simplicity and inner peace (which are achieved by reason and choice, independent of religion), and a general word for the greatest happiness possible, in which the gods might land you through their favoritism or your bribery of them.

The Epicureans had preached that people should sacrifice their ambitions and passions for a calm state of mind, walk away from business and politics and love affairs, get only the things they needed to stay alive, and enjoy simple pleasures. The classic expression of this is in the epic poem of Lucretius, *On the Nature of the Universe:* it is delightful to see, from the safe, calm land, a ship struggling through a storm, or to witness a battle on a distant plain—or to watch people chasing money, fame, and power when you are doing no such thing.

But the Greeks and Romans in general thought that the gods alone, not a person's own choices, were powerful enough to create a winner, in this world or the next. Here is a hymn to Earth, of uncertain date, but probably from the fifth century B.C. or earlier:

You give lush fields and lovely children, lady.
You give and take the livelihood of humans.
Whoever your heart honors with its kindness
Is happy—all things lavishly are his.
Crops weigh his fields down, cattle crowd his meadows,
And fine possessions overflow his mansion.
Earth's favorites rule by good laws over cities
Of lovely women; splendid wealth attends them.
Their sons thrive in exuberance and pleasure.
Their joyful virgin daughters leap and scamper
In flower-draped troupes on softly blooming meadows.
This is your favor, holy, generous goddess.

So what was this preacher, this man called Paul, trying to do? He wrote that if you could, you should detach yourself and get out of the rat race, but also that you should go way beyond what the Epicureans advised: if you could manage, you should actually not get married, and if you were married, you shouldn't let it control so much of what you did and thought (even if you were a woman). But wait: what simple pleasures outside the rat race were there without a home and family? Lucretius certainly wasn't detached from a desire for these; he offered particularly anxious instructions for begetting the "cute children" anyone was supposed to be unhappy without.

Wait again. Paul claimed that what he had to offer was much better than adorable children and a good night's sleep, better even than conventional people's version of the greatest happiness: a rich household with glorious progeny, and reputation, power, and wealth to hand on to them—which all, by the way, was also mainly about marriage. And he preached that bliss beyond this didn't come to a few by the whims of the gods, but could come to anyone because it *was* God: you got bliss from keeping yourself open to him.

Paul did make a huge change in the status of women and in marriage, but not the one we ascribe to him. By bringing the question of happiness into it, he let loose not only that hope and possibility, but with it all of the complexity that ancient customs had tamped down. People now had to figure out relationships between the sexes: whether to have relationships at all, whether they bring too much pain and trouble, whether something else would be more fulfilling, how to balance relationships with the spiritual life, and how to love each other selflessly rather than take each other for granted as providers and breeders. It's lucky that Christians counted on divine help, because they were going to need it.

Say that a fictional woman in Greek or Roman literature—Cydippe, for example—were a Christian, and her fate were not marshaled along by gods representing nature and state authority. Acontius is in love with her, ties notes to little gifts and throws them through her window, talks to her parents, who like him but are not going to pressure her. She is drawn to him in turn, but she is attached to praying in the *ekklēsia.* She sees her mother kept at home by the younger children, while her father can go to any meetings he likes. Her parents struggle to be friends. They care for each other, but different things interest them.

She asks God what she should do, and he does not answer except to say that he loves her enough to have handed his son to murderers for her sake. She is really going to have to make this decision, and she will never be able to blame anyone else for it. Nothing is made up about her life, nothing is written: no fate, no dynasty, no adventures she must produce heroes for but cannot come along on. She has life more abundantly than women before her have ever had it, the shock of it, the glaring light of it. This is what God gave her: all hers, and eternal.

CHAPTER 5: JUST FOLLOWING ORDERS? PAUL AND THE STATE

Paul's famous passage on obedience to government officials, Romans 13:1–7, creates almost unanimous discomfort for Christians, and outright hostility in some others.

> 1 Let every person be subject to the governing
> authorities: for there is no authority except from God,
> and those authorities that exist have been instituted by
> God. 2 Therefore whoever resists authority resists what
> God has appointed, and those who resist will incur
> judgment. 3 For rulers are not a terror to good con-
> duct, but to bad. Do you wish to have no fear of the
> authority? Then do what is good, and you will receive
> its approval; 4 for it is God's servant for your good. But
> if you do what is wrong, you should be afraid, for the
> authority does not bear the sword in vain! It is the
> servant of God to execute wrath on the wrongdoer.
> 5 Therefore one must be subject, not only because of
> wrath but because of conscience. 6 For the same reason

> you also pay taxes, for the authorities are God's servants, busy with this very thing.
> 7 Pay to all what is due to them—taxes to whom taxes are due, revenue to whom revenue is due, respect to whom respect is due, honor to whom honor is due.

Paul's command to Christians simply to obey anyone set over them seems to take away all checks on the state doing evil. Here, for example, is a way Saint Augustine (late fourth–early fifth century A.D.) used the passage, setting out ideas that would prop up the Crusades and the Spanish Inquisition. The Latin words for "lawful authority" and "placed under" look as if they come from Paul's Greek:

> For when a soldier has been lawfully placed under any authority, and obeys it in killing someone, he does not have to answer to a charge of murder under any law of his government. In fact, unless he goes through with the killing, he will have to answer to a charge of treason—deliberate treason. But if he did it on his own impulse and by his own authority, he would be accused of spilling human blood. So it is for the same reason [defiance of lawful authority] that he is punished both if he kills without an order and if he ignores an order and does not kill.

Later thinkers just ran amok. I found, for example, a pamphlet from 1647 entitled *The Magistrates Authority, in Matters of Religion; And the Souls Immortality, Vindicated in two* ***SERMONS*** *Preach'd at York, By Christopher Cartvvright, B.D. and Minister of Gods Word there.*

The first {sermon} was occasioned by the contrary tenet of some which had relation to the Army, who being in the City of York (where this worthy Minister Mr Cartwright *resides) there indeavored to maintain, that the Magistrate hath no power to punish or restrain any that shal vent never so false doctrines & heretical opinions; which stirred up the zeal of this Reverend Divine to choose that Text,* Rom 13.4. *of purpose, and to handle the point* ex professo [avowedly], *as thou mayst perceive by the ensuing Sermon, . . .*

Mr. Coleman *preaching before the Parliament said, none but they had to do in the government of the Church; M.* Dell *told them, they had nothing at all to do in reforming the Church; M.* Arrowsmith *said before them, some took the middle way between the two extreams; I have declared my opinion elsewhere concerning the power of the Civil Magistrate in these things; I shal only here add the determination of two reverend Divines, who cannot but be Authentick with the opposers of this truth. The first is* Dr Ames *who propounding this question,* An Haeretici sint a civili Magistratu puniendi, *whether Hereticks be to be punisht by the civil Magistrate; thus answers, 1. That Hereticks are to be suppressed by all godly men according to that calling & power which they have received from God. 2. That the place and office of the Magistrate requires that he suppress wicked disturbers with the sword or the puplick and external power, if need be; quoting those two places* Rom 13.4. 1 Tim. 2.2 [a letter no longer attributed to Paul by the majority of scholars].

3. If the Hereticks be manifest and publickly noxious, they ought by the Magistrate publickly to be punished. 4. If they be manifestly blasphemous and obstinate in those blasphemies, they may also be capitally punisht.

Had enough? So how do we pry such opinions apart from Paul? One crowbar is, of course, Christ's command (which Paul echoes even while stressing obedience to the state) to give to Caesar the things that are Caesar's, but to God the things that are God's (Matthew 22:21). State authorities should get only what is *due* to them, the apostle writes.

On what other principle than this could Paul have explained his own public conduct? Would he have stated that he had gone under interrogation and into prison and before magistrates again and again and received multiple authoritative beatings—three with the official "rods" of the Roman state (2 Corinthians 11:24–25)—because he couldn't stop doing wrong? "Martyr" is Greek for "witness in court"; early Christian martyrs' defining act was to defy authorities formally and face-to-face. Paul must have allowed for this exception. It was his experience that it was not always possible for a Christian to please those placed over him.

But his view of government in the form of the Roman Empire may not have been bad on the whole. While he grew up, Tarsus was thriving as a peaceful provincial capital. If anyone persecuted Jews there, we don't know about it. He lived his entire life, in fact, in an era of relative order and safety following the Roman civil wars: crime was not allowed to grow chaotic enough to embarrass Rome; there were no local potentates doing whatever they wanted; and no wars were being fought except on the edges of the empire. Paul could walk into a town on a well-maintained road and buy a snack at the marketplace and not be reflexively mugged or swindled because he was a stranger: Roman or Roman-type officers ensured that the place was minimally hospitable, that the scales and measuring cups were standard, and that anyone who was aggrieved had some recourse. (If trade didn't work, Rome got no taxes. Trade therefore worked, and this made for an easier life for everyone but the menial slaves producing the goods.) Even more important, it was local Roman officials who, time after time, rescued Paul from fanatical mobs.

Most important of all, in the late fifties, when the epistle to the Romans was written, the teenage emperor Nero was under tutelage and quite well behaved. It was not until 64 A.D. that he connived to start the great fire, for which he blamed and persecuted Christians, making human torches out of them, among other tortures. This was the first of the systematic Roman persecutions. Had I been Paul at this earlier period I would also have thought, "People should just obey, unless they really can't."

But he was addressing himself to people who had a much more vexed view of these matters. First of all, there wasn't any realism or moderation in their feelings about the state. It wasn't useful-but-not-God; it was divine (involving the worship of state gods in state temples, often on behalf of the state) but pretty useless. The state hadn't stopped the civil wars; it had started them and kept them going. It couldn't make anyone obey when it wasn't looking, and sometimes not then. It was like a weak parent of immature children who could not get beyond their fantasies of an all-powerful parent someday solving their problems, and in particular stopping them from hammering one another at every opportunity.*

Like such children, they didn't take any responsibility for their own rescue. I love them to death—did they ever

*Some historical biblical commentaries mention the tax rioting in Puteoli and the persecution of Jews in Rome that might have been going on among Christians themselves at the very time Paul wrote the letter to the Romans.

write entertaining books. But were they born in barns? Would they have jumped off cliffs if somebody had told them not to? True, many of their leaders did not deserve their trust, but where was the chance for improvement when hardly any leaders, no matter how brilliant or conscientious, got any cooperation except in exchange for bribes?

Political satire is just about the most fun among all Greco-Roman literary creations, because it matches our own political satire in wildness and loopiness. The only thing that checks my enjoyment of it is the realization of how serious it was underneath. It was not for people who didn't litter but were skeptical about politicians and liked to blow off steam (like most of us). It was about people like the Athenians, who, when they were supposed to be gathering for the citizens' assembly in the morning, ran around gossiping and goofing off and had to be herded together with a rope, like frisky goats.

I could cite many scenes in Aristophanes, but I've chosen this one from *Lysistrata* because I have my own translation at hand. A magistrate and his attendants are trying to oust rebel women from the Acropolis, where they have seized the national shrine and the state treasury.

COUNCILOR: I AM A COUNCILOR. It is my JOB
To find the wood for oars and PAY FOR IT.
And now these WOMEN shut the gates on me!
It's no good standing here. Those crowbars, quick!
I'll separate these women from their gall.
(A slave is indecisive.)
Hey, slack-jaw, move! What are you waiting for?
You're looking for a pub where you can hide?

Both of you, put these levers in the gates
From that side, and from here I'll stick mine in
And help you shove.

(Lysistrata emerges from the stage building.)

LYSISTRATA: Right, you can shove those bars.
It doesn't take a tool to bring me out.
You don't need siege equipment here. Just brains.

COUNCILOR: Really, you walking poo? Where *is* that guard?
Grab her and tie her hands behind her back.

LYSISTRATA: By Artemis, if that state property's
Fingertip touches me, I'll make him wail.

(Guard backs away.)

COUNCILOR: You're scared of her? Grab her around the waist,
And you—look sharp and help him tie her hands.

(Old Woman #1 enters from door.)

OLD WOMAN #1: Pandrosus help me. Lay one cuticle
On her, and I shall beat you till you shit.

(The two guards slink off.)

COUNCILOR: Such language! Where'd the other archer go?
Get this one first. Just hear that potty mouth!

OLD WOMAN #2: By Phosphorus, one hangnail grazes her,
And you'll be nursing eyes as black as tar.

(Third guard retreats.)

COUNCILOR: What *is* this? Where's a guard? Get hold of her!
One little expedition's at an end.

(Old Woman #3 enters from door.)

OLD WOMAN #3: Go near her, by Tauropolus, and I
Will give you screaming lessons on your hair.
(Fourth guard makes himself scarce.)
COUNCILOR: Now I'm in deep. I've got no archers
left.
We can't let women have the final stomp!

On the Roman side, the repressions of the early empire couldn't impose silence. Stroppy voices rose at the slightest chance. After Claudius's death, the philosopher Seneca, tutor of the new young emperor, Nero, wrote a cruel skit called *The Pumpkinification of the Divine Claudius,* making fun at the same time of the deification of all dead emperors and of this particular emperor, with whom there seems to have been little wrong besides procedural highhandedness, pedantic abstraction, and disabilities, including a limp and a stutter:

> His last words on earth were heard after a noise blared out of that organ from which he spoke more easily. "Alas, I emit the opinion that I have shat myself." I don't actually know whether he did do it. He certainly did it to the rest of the world.

Claudius makes his way to heaven, where he gets a nasty reception from the divine senate. Finally,

> Gaius Caesar* appeared and proceeded to claim him as a slave, producing witnesses who had seen him getting beaten silly by said claimant with the scourge, rods and

*Caligula, his predecessor.

> fists. He was made over to Gaius Caesar, who gave him to Aeacus.* Aeacus gave him to Menander his freedman, to work up prosecutions.

Nero got his in turn, while still alive, from the poet Lucan, who under cover of a flattering epic dedication taunted the squinty and overweight ruler: When you take your place in heaven, don't make it where you have to look at us with "oblique eye/star," or where you'll unbalance the universe. *Versus quadratus* (square verse) and other barely extant popular genres suggest that irreverence went right down the social scale, as it plainly had in the Greek world with the populist satires of Old Comedy—though the Roman Empire was not going to pay for its own skewering, as the Athenian government had done through the dramatic festivals.

Again, modern readers need to imagine the Greeks and Romans *living* these attitudes. It was fun to send up officials because it was also fun to walk over them whenever you could get away with it.

How on earth was Paul going to talk to his Romans about authority? He did need to talk to them, or they would never form orderly communities, let alone work out a conscientious relationship with the state, let alone conceive of a God who, in asking for obedience, wanted nothing but their good. I would have gone back to Tarsus and opened a tent bargain warehouse. Paul emphasized the single part of the state, the army, that nearly everyone respected, though he himself had never been a soldier.†

The strongest thematic word stem in this passage, form-

*A jungle of the dead in the underworld.

†At the time, Jews were exempt from military service.

ing a kind of rough frame, is *tass-*. The stem's basic image is the lining up of armies for battle,* and in this passage the stem occurs in the verbs translated as "be subject" (twice; literally, "be deployed under"), "have been instituted" ("have been deployed through"), "resists" ("is deployed against"), and "has appointed" ("has deployed through").

Greco-Roman literature about the military shows how much reverence Paul was able to tap into with this vocabulary. Whereas we usually think of armies from the outside, in terms of the damage they do, the mainstream Greco-Roman reader evidently thought of them from the inside, as his community's chief tool for survival and prosperity. And whereas our minds jump from military service to dying, the Greeks and Romans would merely have shrugged: you would not be able to refuse military service and the chance of an honored death without choosing a shameful living death. As far as I have read, in many types of accounts, there was no such thing as conscientious objection. Certainly not all free males ended up serving, but for men of any standing, training to serve was unavoidable.† More important for most of Paul's male followers, joining the Roman army was the best deal in the empire, a way for fit, tough, and disciplined provincials to get what they were not born to: Roman citizenship (often

*The Bible itself is an excellent basis for establishing the meaning of *tass-*. In 1 Corinthians 15:23–28, for example, about the return of Christ, Paul uses words from *tass-* for God *deploying* the forces of good, including Christ, and other words for God's army *putting down* the forces of evil.

†No one could even opt out because of a disability, unless he mutilated himself or a boulder fell on him at the age of twelve or something: all imperfect babies were supposed to be exposed, eliminating any who would grow up unfit for service.

just through joining up), careers and status (through promotion), and wealth (through plunder).

Civilians certainly made fun of soldiers. Plautus's Roman comedy *The Bragging Soldier,* from the late third or early second century B.C., depicts an ego-blinded, thickheaded bruiser. But Americans make fun of athletes in the same way, without taking anything away from most boys' fantasies of athletic glory. Athletes are targets of humor in the first place because they are culture heroes. Satire directed at them is of a very different order from political satire.*

By this period, soldierly duty was far from identical to respect for the state. Soldiers were more loyal to their commanders than to the polity, which is just one reason that, say, a U.S. marine in World War II or the Korean War would not have admired them. But for most of a millennium Greeks and Romans in battle formation had been disciplined, self-sacrificing, brilliant in their bravery and energy, unstoppable. A superior battle line was the main reason Alexander had left behind far-flung empires, and the main reason the Roman Empire existed now. The battle line is an extremely important idea in Romans 13, where Paul draws on old ideas of military service for common benefit and on lasting esteem for the military, putting forward a new ethic of shared, responsible authority.

He uses the same image of battle order for the whole hier-

*The soldier is an important piece of the puzzle of pederasty in the ancient world (see chapter 3). A brave, strong, assertive man, a man who took what he wanted, could also take things for the benefit of the community. This was one reason that his manliness (*andreia* [Greek] or *virtus* [Latin]) got more or less a free pass, even when it led to his sodomizing little boys.

archy and any defiance of it: for God setting in place state authorities, who in turn set in place the populace, some of whom set themselves wrongly against the state. This is in fact a lot like warfare on the part of a Greek city-state in the iconic period of Greece's ascendancy: the general elected or appointed not from within the military but from outside and above, by civil authorities, who had as much control over the army as they practically could; and the general sending the army onto the field with the just expectation of 100 percent obedience. In a typical Greek engagement, not only disloyalty or cowardice but excess of zeal or an insistence on showing off could do as much damage as an enemy could, putting comrades—or the whole city—at risk of captivity, enslavement, or death. On this occasion, the Greeks put ego and competition wholly aside.

They had to. The hoplite (probably meaning "heavily armed") line, several men thick, with a wall of shields in front of each rank, moving together to a loud war song and often engaging in a shoving match with the enemy, was the engine of the army. The general depended on soldiers' being aware of their common vulnerability and keeping in the assigned formation as far as they could. Technologically, strategically, and politically he could not have effected a modern type of strict discipline and tight chain of command, even if he had wanted to. He had to trust his men, and they had to trust him.

The fourth-century B.C. general Xenophon narrates how a Greek mercenary army of his own kept order despite the excitement of routing the enemy—notice that he makes no claim to having intervened or directed:

> The two battle lines were within two or three stadia of each other when the Greeks burst into an exultant song

> and began to close with the enemy. As they went forward, a part of the battle line curved backwards,* and those who were left behind broke into a run. And at the same time they gave the traditional battle cry to Ares, and now everyone was running. Some of them say that they pounded their spears against their shields and sent the enemy's horses into a panic. In any case, before an arrow reached them, the barbarians turned and ran. The Greeks pursued with the greatest energy, but at the same time shouted to one another not to make it a stampede but to follow in proper battle rank.

It was hoplite discipline that made Greek mercenary armies prized even after the heyday of the city-states with their citizen armies. This helped the prestige of the battlefield to endure for an extremely long time. And we should also not discount the power of the golden age of Greek warfare in memory. Perhaps the most revered heroes in the entire Greek world were the three hundred Spartans who were doomed from the start in facing off against outrageous numbers of Persians at the pass of Thermopylae in 480 B.C. Their epitaph on the site was "Stranger, go and tell the Spartans that we lie here, obedient to their words." Homeland. Obedience. And the chance to humiliate the god-king Xerxes and claim his glory for their own legacy.

On the Athenian side of reverence for the military is Pericles' oration in honor of the fallen in 431 B.C., probably studied and recited by generations of Greek and Roman schoolboys in the version conveyed by the contemporary historian Thucydides:

*Normal in an attack.

> Giving up their bodies for the common good, they as individuals won praise that never ages, and the most conspicuous burial monument there could be: not the one in which they lie, but the privilege of their glory being remembered forever on every fitting occasion for a word or act to honor it. For the whole earth is the tomb of valiant men. Not only an inscription on pillars in their own land commemorates them, but even in alien countries there lives in every man an unwritten memorial of them, in his heart rather than in material records. Copy them, then, and judge that happiness is freedom and freedom is courage, and pay no attention to the dangers of war.

Here, on the other hand, was the treatment a coward got in a public forum. It is doubtful that Cleonymus actually deserted—he was still around and in public life afterward. But he did lose his shield, which was considered the act of a coward. Aristophanes would never let him forget it. In this scene, a pair of slaves doze and chat while on guard duty in front of a house (their attitude toward a security assignment being notoriously different from that of free men):

> XANTHIAS: Just now I had the most amazing dream. . .
> I thought I saw an eagle,
> A big one, swoop to the public square and grab
> In its claws a snake—no, wait, it was a shield—
> And haul it way up in the sky—but then
> He turned into Cleonymus and dropped it.
> SOSIAS: Cleonymus is that joke now—nothing's
> missing.

XANTHIAS: Whaddaya mean?
SOSIAS: Somebody at a drinking party shouts,
"What kind of animal is it on land
And sea *and* sky—that throws its shield away?"

To sum up the Greek experience, ever since they had real citizen armies (as opposed to pirate bands), they saw conformity and self-sacrifice in warfare as unequivocally good. And though the strategy or even the necessity of a given war might be (in fact, nearly always was) disputed as a matter of public policy, it went unquestioned that the army itself had to exist and be used somehow. Pacifism seems never to have gone further than the question "Why aren't we fighting barbarians rather than our neighbors, who are fellow Greeks?" And though, in practice, the politics of a war could stretch out from the city and into the army on campaign in ways that would shock modern officers, no one ever excused anyone for betraying his comrades on the actual battlefield.

THE ROMAN ARMY, that most important tool of a megalomaniac state, had its own development, but the differences, with their obvious advantages on the ground, would only have given Paul's theme more force for a Roman audience. The Roman army was basically a hoplite one, but instead of one dense line, Romans had distinct layers that could advance and fall back through one another, and instead of one main type of foot soldier, they had four. It would have been impossible to maneuver without more officers, a longer chain of command, and standards to rally to, so Roman military discipline was no joke, much harsher than the discipline in Greek armies, and this difference extended beyond combat.* The Romans, though, placed similar stress on common responsibility and common enforcement. For example, Romans in Rome had neither stoning nor any other gang-up punishment for civilian crime, but Roman soldiers in the field sometimes had to ceremonially stone their derelict comrades.

Not even paternal affection was supposed to overcome military discipline. A famous early general had his son executed for accepting a challenge to duel while he was on guard duty. The breach served to get rid of a leading enemy, but it put individual zeal and ambition above strict obedience. The boy died for being *extra ordinem,* literally "out of the line." (Our word "order" is connected to the Roman battle rank.) Here is the end of the episode according to the historian Livy, and I am not making fun of the style—it really is this lofty.

> "Father," he said, "so that all men may in truth know that you begot me, I bring to you these spoils won from a mounted warrior. The enemy challenged me and I killed him." When the consul heard this, he instantly turned from his son and ordered that the assembly be called by a trumpet blast. When the crowd had gathered, he spoke: "Titus Manlius, since you showed no awe either for the consul's position of command nor for the lofty dignity of a father, and against our command left your post to fight the enemy, and, as far as was in your power, dissolved the military discipline by which the Roman state has stood fast up to

*Xenophon tells of a Greek mercenary army getting away with stoning an allied general for punishing one man unfairly.

> this day, and have drawn me into the necessity of forgetting either the Republic or myself, we must rather be punished for our crime than allow the Republic to pay so dear a price for our sins. 'Tis an austere precedent, but a wholesome one for the youth of the future. I am moved not only by the inborn love of my children but by this indication of bravery—off the mark though it was in its empty display of valor. But given that the authority of the consuls must be either sanctified by your death or revoked forever by your impunity, I would not judge that even you, if you are indeed of my loins, would refuse to restore the military discipline that has toppled through your fault. Guard, tie him to the post."

The army was horrified and protested the young man's death—but Livy writes that the long-term results were just as intended.

Horace revels in the image of the tough, disciplined, self-sacrificing young soldier. He is the professional athlete of the age, riveting spectators (in the poem that Wilfred Owen cites for the "old Lie" of the line about sacrificing life for the fatherland):

> *Let hard war service make a young boy strong;*
> *Narrow privations ought to be his friend.*
> *Let him learn how to be a fearsome horseman,*
> *Harrying the wild Parthians with his spear.*
>
> *His life should run beneath the open sky,*
> *In risky action. From the enemy walls*

The warring tyrant's wife should watch. Beside her
The marriageable young girl ought to sigh,

"The prince I'm promised to is new to warfare.
I hope he won't harass this touchy lion
Whose bloody rage is hurrying him on,
Whipping him through the center of the slaughter."

Death for the fatherland is sweet and proper,
Since death runs down the runaway as well.
It doesn't spare the timid back and hamstrings
Of any youth who's indisposed to war.

Did the Romans ever see someone who was marked out as a coward surviving in public life, if only for perpetual taunting, like the Athenian Cleonymus? Glad you asked. No.

As I've indicated, by Paul's time the Roman army had long since evolved from a body of native citizens to a mercenary force packed with foreigners. It is endlessly disputable whether the Roman citizen-soldier or the barbarian professional was better. But the late-republican or imperial soldier, sent on lengthy campaigns against astute insurgent savages on the frontiers, in appalling climates and terrains where the supply lines would often fail, had to be a machine, because that was how he was used; and the soldier's new status as universal guardian and enforcer, with all of its perks, was probably worth quite some performance to hang on to. Petronius's antihero Encolpius, who doesn't respect much, can accept that it is a good thing to be stopped by a real soldier from acting as a pretend one because of a private spat. Here the pompous language is, in effect, stolen from the military. Self-indulgent, criminal, and pretentious, Encolpius cannot be more than a parody of a soldier.

> "Now the lovers are lying entwined all night long, and maybe when the demands of their mutual lust leave them exhausted, they mock my solitude. But they won't get away with it. Either I'm no man, or no free man, or else I'm going to offer guilty blood as a sacrifice to the wrong I've suffered."
>
> This said, I girded on a sword and, lest bodily weakness hinder my soldiering, I enlivened my strength by food in large quantities. Then I leapt out into the street and dashed around every portico like a madman. My face was frenzied and savage, my mind full of nothing but blood and murder, and I kept bringing my hand to the pommel of the sword I had consecrated to revenge. A soldier—just an impostor, a hoodlum after dark, I'm sure—noticed me and said, "Hey, buddy, how is it? Which legion are you from? Whose century?"
>
> Very collectedly, I made up a number and a name, but he answered, "What army are you talking about, where soldiers go around in dancing shoes?" At this point the lie also began to show on my face and in my general air of fear. He ordered me to down arms and watch out or he'd give me a thrashing. Despoiled—even worse, my revenge cut short—I returned to my lodging, and as my impetuous mood sagged I began to give thanks for the thug's arrogance.

Even more important, at this period we get a lot of evidence from the horse's mouth, confirming that even the rank and file honored the military. Leaders and their pet writers *would* report how good it was to be a soldier. But the dry climates of the Middle East preserve letters home of provincial recruits who were proud and content to serve. And why not? Where else could they get the opportunities they had?

To make a thousand-year story very short, the Greeks and Romans had a high regard for military service: it was for them a vital, prestigious duty. And they didn't regard fighting as the big drawback in a military career: a battle was the best part, the chance to prove what they were made of and win a lifetime's worth of benefits—or more: perhaps even a land allotment they could pass on to their children.

So when Paul wrote about "subjection" in military language, the images his readers had were *not* of shoveling manure or being beaten into submission. They were of respected, rewarded functions. He was in effect urging his followers to become stakeholders, leaders themselves through their cooperation.

SINCE THE ARMY was the part of government that could really work, protecting and enriching the people, many polytheistic authors show that in civic life, people should behave like good soldiers. "Staying where you were posted"—that is, in the assigned position in the line—was an apt metaphor for public responsibility. Plato's Socrates boasts at his trial about his steadiness in battle, comparing it to his steadiness in serving the state through his philosophical inquiries. Ironically, he is now serving the state against its will, but he claims (and generations of readers admiringly accepted) that a god had assigned him to do this. (Compare Paul's picture of God, the state, and good private individuals acting for a unanimous purpose.) In this passage, Plato has a little orgy with *tasso,* the archetypal verb for posting or deploying:

> So this is the truth of the matter, Athenian gentlemen. Wherever somebody chooses, after due consideration, to best deploy himself, or wherever he is deployed by a leader, it seems to me that he has to stay there and take his chances like anybody else, regarding neither death nor anything else as more important than the chance that he could disgrace himself. Men of Athens, when the leaders you chose to have charge of me deployed me at Potidea and Amphipolis and Delium, I stayed where they deployed me, like anybody else. It would be abominable if, when a god had deployed me, as I thought and believed, and made me spend my life seeking insight and examining myself and others, I should in that position get into a panic over death or anything else at all and leave my post.

Government itself should be as much like the military as possible, many thought. Several Greek writers of the fourth and fifth centuries B.C. admired the barracks state Sparta, without having a marked desire to live there themselves. According to an outside account, Spartan men needed to sneak out of the common mess hall to consummate their marriages. They could not raise their own children—neither could the mothers, who had to surrender them to boot camp when they reached what would be grade school age these days. But they never saw anything as prissy as boots there, and like their sisters, they drilled semi-naked.

Plato in his *Republic,* about the ideal state, does not cringe in arguing for a totalitarian military regime to address the conflicts with neighbors that must follow any full development of a civilized town. In his utopia, experts ("guardians," compared to guard dogs) would employ people wherever they could serve best, with no regard to individual wants. Discipline and self-sacrifice must be perfect—even in following regulations for musical composition and performance. Plato imagined that a people trained and led in such a way would be undefeatable.

For the Romans, republican government, with its strained, breaking efforts to keep the civil power separate, had meant a hundred years of civil wars. A military regime now meant peace at home. Once the army was in control there, it could turn its violent work outward. Yea!

In the *Aeneid,* Vergil's hero Aeneas, on his way to found Rome, visits the underworld, where his dead father points out the souls of great Romans to be born in the future, including the civil warriors Julius Caesar and Pompey; the father decries them and thrills at how much better the militant empire will be:

> *"See those two in bright matched armor,*
> *Souls in accord while Night imprisons them.*
> *But once they reach the light, how great a war*
> *They'll rouse, what ranks of slaughter, father-in-law*
> *Come down the bouldered Alps from high Monoecus,*
> *And son-in-law deploying all the East.*
> *Children, don't lose your horror of such warfare.*
> *Don't turn your massive strength against your country.*
> *You of the gods' stock: take the lead, have mercy!*
> *My son, throw down your weapons! . . .*
> *Others, I know, will beat out softer-breathing*
> *Bronze shapes, or draw from marble living faces,*

> *Excel in pleading cases, chart the sky's paths,*
> *Predict the rising of the constellations.*
> *But Romans, don't forget that world dominion*
> *Is your great craft: peace, and then peaceful customs;*
> *Sparing the conquered, striking down the haughty."*

Even in Paul's time, under Nero, people deplored the civil wars and rejoiced in the empire. Lucan devoted an entire (and pretty terrible) epic poem to this, narrating the past conflicts with enflamed melodrama:

> *I sing of civil wars sweeping Emathia's plains—*
> *License given to crime—a powerful people*
> *Driving victorious weapons through their own guts—*
> *Kindred battle lines—a pact of kingship broken—*
> *All power in the battered world contesting*
> *In shared atrocity. . . .*

In summary, by using military words, Paul takes perhaps the only path there was to convincing Greeks and Romans that it would be useful to obey all state authorities. He draws on the firm and widespread belief that the military was where an individual got real standing and respect for serving the state. And Paul taps into actual experience that, as far as governance was good, it was military. And he concentrates on the most unambiguously respected part of the military: the conventional battle line, where mutual support and individual survival were the same project.

In the passage quoted from Romans, other words besides the *tass-* compounds have military meanings, such as the words translated as "good" and "bad." They weren't usually so abstract in their connotations. The basic idea of *agathos* is "brave" or "noble," and of *kakos,* "cowardly" or "worthless." (There are other words than *agathos* for a slave or a tyrant's subject who is behaving himself.)

Even when using words for civil authority, Paul selects those that support the idea of willing, rational duty. There are plenty of words in Greek for power and position, but Paul chose (and used four times) *exousia,* a word for deserving authority. "Authorities" is from an abstract, feminine singular noun, as if the people in charge are just containers for a quality coming from God. The NRSV, which I quote here, rightly calls state authority "it."

The other names for leaders here are *archontes,* which is the ordinary word for "magistrates," and *diakonos,* translated as "servant." This is no mere slave or lowly servant but, among other functions, a messenger or the attendant at a religious ceremony. Paul applies this word to his special assistants—in modern terms, the church deacons.

A more contextual translation of *syneidesis* (NRSV: "conscience") would be better. Why is "conscience" as well as fear supposed to make us obey? We often think of conscience as the inner voice that urges us to stand up to authority. Actually, the Greek word is closer to "conscientiousness"—literally "knowing with," originally about communication, and far more like a dutiful feeling for the common good than an inner voice different from what other people are saying.

Another important word here is *opheilai* ("debts," translated as "what is due"). It is used only once, but it covers a range of things: taxes (ordinary tribute), revenue (excise taxes), respect, and honor. Near the center of polytheistic public ethics (such as they were) was monetary debt, which the debtor swore on oath to pay,* so that he feared divine vengeance as well as the loss of his property and reputation (even freedom, in earlier times) should he default. To keep your self-respect, and to do anything else worth doing, you had to pay your debts. A freedman in Petronius, in furious and comic slang, rants at people making fun of him:

> "I hope I live a life that don't make me nobody's joke. I'm a man good as any other, walk with my head high and don't hide from nobody. I don't owe a red cent. Nobody hauls me into court, nobody stops me in the forum and says, 'Pay up!'"

Christianity deepened and expanded the concept of debt. I mentioned in chapter 4 (pp. 106–07) that Paul elevates the marriage relationship (and the status of wives) by applying the word to sex. In parables and in the Lord's Prayer (how many readers know the older—literal—translation, "Forgive us our debts as we forgive our debtors"?), it is a metaphor for sin. The word moves from commerce to personal life and the life of the Spirit, since Christians must have a fuller sense of obligation.

But Paul wants even more for leaders: "respect" and "honor" (a synonym for "elective or appointed office"). And he's not done. There's even more in Romans 13:

> 8 Owe no one anything, except to love one another;
> for the one who loves another has fulfilled the law. 9
> The commandments, "You shall not commit adultery;
> You shall not murder; You shall not steal; You shall not
> covet"; and any other commandment, are summed up
> in this word, "Love your neighbor as yourself." 10 Love
> does no wrong to a neighbor; therefore love is the ful-
> filling of the law.

Public duty is about love.

Oops. Through a contextual reading, I come not to an out, not to an endorsement of my own civic values by Paul. I find instead a challenge to complete them or move beyond them. I have to adopt an even harder standard of love than in the familiar Old Testament and gospel commands to care for the weak. What a charming thing to be able to do once in a while. What a firm proof of both my power and my goodness. To show sympathy and sincere deference to those with power over me, to trust them with my life as if on a battlefield and forgive the very costly mistakes they make, is harder. It's like managing to love my damn parents.

Don't let me start in about them—not that I need to. I know the sterility of not seeing state authorities as human beings or appreciating their goodwill. I've ripped into Nelson Mandela.

There the article is for eternity, that stain on my Google, the fruit of a brand-new Harvard Ph.D. plopped down in Africa to teach Latin and Greek right after apartheid ended. I wouldn't back down from the article even when a Quaker elder e-mailed me, appalled and asking whether my tone was helpful, regardless of what the facts were. Instead of repenting, I busied myself with showing how enlightened and compassionate I was. And I *was*! One of the students I taught as a volunteer told a career counselor that she wanted to be Sarah Ruden. I figured out a way to keep a family of eight from starving while their breadwinner was in the hospital with a knife wound. I was right, I was good, while these Africans who had barged into the government, even the so-called best of them—

If God managed to love me enough to sacrifice his Son, I have to manage with political leaders: nude in public except for signs that say, "Imagine how much better you would look," wide open to self-righteous hatred, wanting more power but needing love from those they can kill with the flick of a gold pen. It's just hopeless.

Or maybe not. God came through for Paul sometimes. One of the times is on record in Acts 17:

> 16 While Paul was waiting for them in Athens, he was deeply distressed to see that the city was full of idols. 17 So he argued in the synagogue with the Jews and the devout persons, and also in the marketplace every day with those who happened to be there. 18 Also some Epicurean and Stoic philosophers debated with him. Some said, "What does this babbler want to say?" Others said, "He seems to be a proclaimer of foreign divinities." (This was because he was telling the good news about Jesus and the resurrection.) 19 So they took him and brought him to the Areopagus* and asked him, "May we know what this new teaching is that you are presenting? 20 It sounds rather strange to us, so we would like to know what it means.". . .
>
> 22 Then Paul stood in front of the Areopagus and said, "Athenians, I see how extremely religious you are in every way. 23 For as I went through your city and looked carefully at the objects of your worship, I found among them an altar with the inscription, 'To an unknown god.' What therefore you worship as unknown, this I proclaim to you. 24 The God who made the world and everything in it, he who is Lord of heaven and earth, does not live in shrines made by

*This was the government council that dealt with religious crimes.

> human hands, 25 nor is he served by human hands, as
> though he needed anything, since he himself gives to
> all mortals life and breath and all things. 26 From one
> ancestor he made all nations to inhabit the whole earth,
> and he allotted the times of their existence and the
> boundaries of the places where they would live, 27 so
> that they would search for God and perhaps grope for
> him and find him—though indeed he is not far from
> each one of us."

But it takes *faith* to come up with something as insouciantly ingenious as that. I could start to love my parents, and to deal with them, when I wasn't afraid of them anymore, when I knew they didn't have any power over me that mattered. I can love authority and reach out to it when I've put it in the right place, as in Romans 8, where all of the things that work on the universe, or seem to work on it, slide into the one word "Lord"—*kyrios,* "the one in charge":

> 37 No, in all these things we are more than con-
> querors through him who loved us. 38 For I am con-
> vinced that neither death, nor life, nor angels, nor
> rulers, nor things present, 39 nor things to come, nor
> powers, nor height, nor depth, nor anything else in all
> creation, will be able to separate us from the love of
> God in Christ Jesus our Lord.

CHAPTER 6: NOBODY HERE BUT US BONDSMEN: PAUL ON SLAVERY

Paul's pronouncements on slavery are in a class by themselves, among all of his writings that have caused controversy in the modern world. On other matters, he gives straightforward advice and orders, and only a perverse reading can muddle the substance of his program. What this program meant to his readers and what it should mean to us are the only crucial questions remaining. Not so with slavery, and this is disturbing. The institution is sparse today, at least in the industrialized world, but it used to be mankind's great crime, as genocide is now. We really *want* Paul to have been against slavery, but the evidence is galling. It's not that he was *for* slavery; it's quite unlikely that he wrote Ephesians 6:5–8, for example, which exhorts slaves to submit and serve wholeheartedly. It's that he doesn't seem to have cared one way or another. Key verses are 1 Corinthians 7:21–23, in which he states that slavery is nothing, that slaves should just get on with their religious lives.

I spent a day at the Library of Congress, in Washington, looking through the writings of people trying to *make* Paul care. I was most interested in nineteenth-century American works on Christianity and slavery, displayed in the catalog as a scrum of titles: *Slavery condemned by Christianity, Slavery consistent with Christianity, Slavery and the slaveholders' religion; as opposed to Christianity,* and so on. But I already knew some recent studies that dealt with the same topic, including John Dominic Crossan and Jonathan L. Reed's *In Search of Paul.*

Packing up my notes in the evening, I realized that clarity was not going to come from either direction. The newer authors are curiously like the older ones in their attitude, which is that, in the cosmic talk show, Jesus and the apostles are respectfully interviewing them, not the other way around. Time, tragic historical experiences, and loads of fresh empirical data have not made even the academic view of the New Testament more objective. In their own way, present-day biblical scholars are as stubbornly themselves, and as closed to the reality of original Christianity, as both the abolitionists and the plantation owners were.

My frustration settled on interpretations of Paul's letter to Philemon, written on behalf of a runaway slave, which is the main witness to his attitude toward slavery. Here is the entire letter, comprising the shortest book of the Bible:

> 1 Paul, a prisoner of Christ Jesus, and Timothy our
> brother,
> To Philemon our dear friend and co-worker, 2 to
> Apphia our sister, to Archippus our fellow-soldier, and
> to the church in your house:
> 3 Grace to you and peace from God our Father and
> the Lord Jesus Christ.
> 4 When I remember you in my prayers, I always
> thank my God 5 because I hear of your love for all the

saints and your faith towards the Lord Jesus. 6 I pray
that the sharing of your faith may become effective
when you perceive all the good that we may do for
Christ. 7 I have indeed received much joy and encour-
agement from your love, because the hearts of the
saints have been refreshed through you, my brother.

8 For this reason, though I am bold enough in
Christ to command you to do your duty, 9 yet I would
rather appeal to you on the basis of love—and I, Paul,
do this as an old man, and now also as a prisoner of
Christ Jesus. 10 I am appealing to you for my child,
Onesimus, whose father I have become during my
imprisonment. 11 Formerly he was useless to you, but
now he is indeed useful both to you and to me. 12 I am
sending him, that is, my own heart, back to you. 13 I
wanted to keep him with me, so that he might be of
service to me in your place during my imprisonment
for the gospel; 14 but I preferred to do nothing without your consent, in order that your good deed might
be voluntary and not something forced. 15 Perhaps this
is the reason he was separated from you for a while, so
that you might have him back forever, 16 no longer as
a slave but as more than a slave, a beloved brother—
especially to me but how much more to you, both in
the flesh and in the Lord.

17 So if you consider me your partner, welcome him
as you would welcome me. 18 If he has wronged you in
any way, or owes you anything, charge that to my
account. 19 I, Paul, am writing this with my own
hand: I will repay it. I say nothing about your owing
me even your own self. 20 Yes, brother, let me have this

> benefit from you in the Lord! Refresh my heart in
> Christ. 21 Confident of your obedience, I am writing
> to you, knowing that you will do even more than I say.
> 22 One thing more—prepare a guest room for me,
> for I am hoping through your prayers to be restored
> to you.
> 23 Epaphras, my fellow-prisoner in Christ Jesus,
> sends greetings to you, 24 and so do Mark, Aristarchus,
> Demas, and Luke, my fellow-workers.
> 25 The grace of the Lord Jesus Christ be with your
> spirit.

On the basis of these same words, the interpretations diverge as widely, and as wrongheadedly on either side, as in the following passages. The first is from the Reverend Theodore Clapp's "Slavery: A Sermon, Delivered in the First Congregational Church in New Orleans, April 15, 1838":

> The epistle to Philemon was written by Paul, while a prisoner at Rome. Philemon was a slave-holder, residing at Colosse. Onesimus, a fugitive slave belonging to Philemon, was converted to the Christian religion at Rome, under the ministry of Paul. The epistle sends him back to Colosse, with a letter to his owner; in which he entreats Philemon not to punish Onesimus with severity, but to treat him in future as a reformed and faithful slave. . . .
>
> Paul did not suggest to Philemon the duty of emancipating Onesimus, but encouraged him to restore the slave to his former condition, with the hope that, acting under the influence of the holy principles of Christianity, he would in future serve his master, "not

with eye service," as formerly, "but in singleness of heart, fearing God."

Crossan gets an opposite message out of the same text:

> Delicately and carefully, but relentlessly and implacably Paul presses home his point. Philemon should free Onesimus. . . . Paul sees an impossible or intolerable opposition between a *Christian* master owning a *Christian* slave. How can they be equal in Christ, but unequal in society? How can they be equal and unequal at the same time? He does not and would never accept the idea that they could be equal spiritually, internally, in the assembly, but unequal physically, externally, in the world. Both are Christians, and they must be equal "both in the flesh and in the Lord" (16).

Crossan at least quotes from the text in question, whereas Clapp seems to call on Colossians 3:22 or Ephesians 6:6, on words that are probably not from Paul and are not at all like the letter to Philemon. But both writers are equally deadpan in asserting something the letter, as it urges Philemon to take the runaway back, absolutely doesn't specify: what this person's legal status should be. In this instance, you just cannot assign a definite meaning to the Greek word *hōs* (in verse 16): "like, as, as if, in the character of, in the capacity of." Should Onesimus be a free man, not continuing *"as"* a slave—or should Philemon merely not treat him *"like"* a slave?

Early Christian theology helps no more than the Greek does to decide this question. Even by the high standards of the gospels, Philemon could have been treating Onesimus "not *hōs* a slave but more than a slave, a beloved brother," if he merely forgave him. Jesus had commanded his followers to forgive their metaphoric "brothers" no matter what, but had not said that they must go beyond forgiveness and upgrade the relationship, whatever it officially was.*

But bare forgiveness was radical enough, especially in the main territory of Paul's mission. There, forgiving a runaway slave (particularly a runaway who had taken goods with him, as Onesimus may have done), instead of sending him to hard labor, branding him, crucifying him, or whipping him to death, was no small matter, when he had so shockingly betrayed his household (*familia* in Latin, from which we have the obvious derivative). Running away and its punishments are the stuff of black comedy. The ancients treated such episodes almost the way we treat sex acts: the details are too shameful for mainstream literature or polite conversation. For the Romans as for us, a single-word insult—for them "runaway"—could invoke adequate disgust on its own.

To show the extremity of what Paul faced in having a runaway slave land in his lap, I will start with a scene in Petronius. Imagine what the apostle got used to in the established Greco-Roman society he experienced, as when he was staying with a man wealthy enough to have a guest room, as Philemon did. Petronius's story of Trimalchio's dinner party is exaggerated and absurd, but the narrator Encolpius provides the voice of cultured common sense among all of the pretentious uproar. From him we know that it was good form for the master to order severe punishment for slaves even in the case of carelessness and accidents that in any way marred

*Note that a parable of a master or "ruler" merely forgiving a servant or dependent a debt directly follows that command at Matthew 18:21–35.

hospitality. It was also apparently polite for the guests to intervene, in the spirit of "Oh no, not on my behalf, please!" But both the master and the guests were entitled to be quite annoyed at anything a slave did to draw attention to himself, and the host Trimalchio's outrageous gaucheness is at its worst when he actually connives for his slaves to play pranks. Here is one incident:

> Before all of the intellectual world had succumbed to the disease of his conversation, a platter with an immense pig on it took over the table. We were struck by the speed of the cooking, and we swore that even a chicken couldn't be done in so short a time. We were even more suspicious in that the pig looked bigger than before. Trimalchio inspected it more and more closely, and burst out, "What the—? This pig isn't gutted! By Hercules, it really isn't!"
>
> The cook stood in front of the table and cringed and said he'd forgotten to gut the pig. "What?! You forgot?! He says it like he just forgot to put in pepper and cumin. Strip him."
>
> In a moment, the cook was stripped and standing between two of the punishment crew. We started to beg him off. "It happens. Please, let him go. If he does it again, none of us will say a word for him." But I, as usual, was feeling intolerant and punitive. I couldn't hold myself back from leaning over and whispering in Agamemnon's ear, "I've never seen such a worthless slave in my life. How could somebody forget to gut a pig? By Hercules, I wouldn't pardon him if it had been a fish he'd forgotten to gut." But Trimalchio's face had relaxed into a grin.

"Okay. Since you can't remember nothin', gut it in front of us."

The slave got his tunic back on, snatched a knife, and jabbed cautiously at the pig's stomach here and there. In no time, the weight of the flesh widened the cuts, and sausages and black puddings began to pour out.

The slaves applauded this trick and shouted, "Long live Gaius!"

To be seen and never heard was not the universal rule. Some slaves gained status in households and entered into close relationships with their masters. Cicero's secretary Tiro is an example. Some masters, like Seneca, vaunted their humanity toward slaves. But I submit that slaves were like pets: good treatment of them was about the masters' enlightenment, never about the slaves' inherent equality. The master was absolutely entitled to keep a slave in line, according to his own convenience. Horace depicts his slave Davus's cornering him and dressing him down during the Saturnalia, the festival that gave slaves broad license; but Davus goes too far:

DAVUS: If a steaming cake tempts *me,* then *I'm* no good.
How can posh dinners suit *your* lofty virtue?
Does my stomach rule me less destructively?
My back gets lashed, but are you punished less
When you go after such expensive food?
Unlimited good things can go quite bitter.
Your put-upon feet balk at carrying
Your bulk. The slave at dusk who steals a scraper
To trade for grapes is *bad.* To sell estates

In service to your belly isn't slavish?
And you can't spend an hour on your own.
You waste time, dodge yourself, a runaway,
A truant hiding out in sleep and wine
From your anxieties.
HORACE: A stone!
DAVUS: Why?
HORACE: Arrows!
DAVUS: He's crazy—or it's poetry.
HORACE: Out of here,
Or you'll join the workers on my Sabine farm.

If women were supposed to be basically wild and lustful, slaves were supposed to be basically naughty, needing, like women, a lot of control. The more quick-witted and adaptable a slave in Plautus, the worse use he makes of his talents, and the more cheerfully unreformable he is. The slave whom the play *Pseudolus (Faker)* is named for sets in motion and controls the action, an elaborate swindle to put his young master in possession of a prostitute girlfriend whom a pimp is about to sell away; the scheme is hardly the noble enterprise it might pass for nowadays. At the end of *The Haunted House,* a slave thumbs his nose at the threat of punishment for making a complete fool of his owner, who is going to stay a fool and forgive him.

TRANIO: Now you've forgiven him—what about me?
THEOPROPIDES: I'll tie you up for a flogging, you
turd.
TRANIO: Though I'm ashamed?
THEOPROPIDES: If I myself survive, I'll kill you.
CALLIDAMATES: You should spread your kindness:

Please, can't you pardon Tranio? Do it for my sake.
THEOPROPIDES: I'd rather you got anything out of me but that.
I've got to grind him into the ground for his horrible crimes.
CALLIDAMATES: Please, let him off.
THEOPROPIDES: You see that thug flaunting at the altar?*
CALLIDAMATES: Tone it down, Tranio—be smart.
THEOPROPIDES: *You* tone it down.
Him I'll tone down with a beating, put him in his place.
TRANIO: Really, there's no need.
CALLIDAMATES: Come on, *please,* give in.
THEOPROPIDES: No, give it up.
CALLIDAMATES: By Hercules, I beg you.
THEOPROPIDES: I beg *you:* stop.
CALLIDAMATES: No point resisting.
Please—just this single, solitary time—do it for me.
TRANIO: What's your problem? As if I won't do something else tomorrow.
Then you can get me good—for either time, for both.

The most subhuman slave was the runaway; his only ties to society had been the uses that real people could make of him, and he now forfeited these ties. He was a little like a raped or adulterous woman, but unlike her he bore all of the loathing and fury, in this case the extreme loathing and fury that come when absolute privilege is disappointed.

As a rule, a runaway was simply a lost cause: a far-out outlaw as long as he could sustain it, and a tortured animal or a

*He has taken refuge at the altar in an attempt to avoid punishment.

carcass when caught. Here is a rare detailed depiction. In Petronius, characters masquerade as caught runaways after they realize they have a choice between being recognized and killed, and becoming objects whose repulsiveness will bar any other impression from onlookers' minds. They shave their heads as part of the disguise, and even after this act has been reported to the owner of the ship on which they are sailing—haircutting at sea was considered a bad omen—and they must stand in the middle of an angry crowd that includes their longtime enemies, their protector still hopes that their role of degradation will shield their identity:

> Lichas was furious. "Somebody cut his hair in my ship— and in the middle of the night? Bring the bastards here. Whoever they are, I'm going to offer their heads to appease the ship's spirit."
>
> "I ordered it," said Eumolpus. "I'm on the same ship, though—I certainly wouldn't intentionally do anything to provoke divine anger. It was only that a pair of condemned slaves of mine had long, shaggy hair, and I didn't want to make the ship look like a prison, so I ordered the matted mess removed. And I also didn't want their hair to cover the writing on their faces; everyone was supposed to see those marks of disgrace. Among their other crimes, they stole money from me and spent it on a shared girlfriend. Last night I dragged them from her house, stinking of perfume and unmixed wine. In a word, they reek of what was left of my family fortune." . . .
>
> To appease the guardian spirit of the ship, it was determined that we should each receive forty lashes. Without delay, the enraged sailors stepped up to us and

> laid in with their ropes, trying to satisfy the god with our blood—our suffering obviously counting for little in this exchange.

Again, who a runaway was—nobody and nothing—tells us who a slave was: nobody and nothing aside from his usefulness. And Aristotle and others indicate that he is inherently that. This is what makes the debate over the letter to Philemon, concentrating on the question of legal freedom, so silly. We are not in the ancient Near East, where the people who were slaves in Egypt become masters in Canaan. Such a change was not conceivable in the polytheistic Roman Empire. Had Philemon freed Onesimus, it would not have turned Onesimus into a full human being. That is what Paul wants, so he does not ask for the tool that won't achieve it.

Manumission did *not* confer citizenship, which contained some rights we consider basic, such as due process and the exemption from cruel punishments. Most important, manumission kept the traditional barriers of the household up and prevented slaves (who might in reality be the master's children) from ever dreaming of competing with legitimate children or other members of the clan. If slaves got their freedom, they went either into permanent subordination or into exile.

The freed slave might stay part of the household and enjoy its support and protection—no small matters in that world—by taking on the status of a dependent. In this case, he would be a sort of servant at large, only partly free, and if he defied his former master, he could be punished or even taken back into slavery. Pliny the Younger, of the late first and early second centuries A.D., wrote a letter of intercession for a *freedman* who had offended his *former* master. Pliny does not specify the offense—it could be nearly anything. The problem is the former master's anger, referred to five times in the short letter, which begins:

> Your freedman, at whom you said you were angry, came to me. He collapsed at my feet and clung to them as if they were yours. He cried a lot, begged a lot, was silent for a long time, and in short convinced me that his repentance was real. I believe he's mended his ways, because he's aware he went wrong.

On the other hand, the freed slave might be completely free, with no obligations—but then the former master would not want him around at all and would never help him. A man of position gave nothing away. Anyone who got food, money, discarded clothes, or even a glance or word from him had to perform rigorous duties as a henchman. Even the freeborn poor, in Roman literature, stumble anxiously through the streets before dawn to join the other "clients" wishing the "patron" good morning. He can send them on virtually any errand, including that of rubbing out somebody else's clients.

Legend has connected this Onesimus, as a freedman, and the Onesimus who was bishop of Ephesus in the early nineties and a martyr. But legends like to grow on texts the way those rain forest plants with aerial roots grow on trees: there is no other support. To apply the proper skepticism, we have to picture Onesimus's options in the real world, as Paul would have pictured them if at any point he considered simply telling Philemon to set the slave free. How would Onesimus have survived? Certainly at this period, the church had no formal, salaried posts. And anyway, who would have accepted as a church authority someone who had once been a runaway slave?

To survive on his own, did he have trade skills, or savings to set up a business? Day laborers tended to be half-starved wretches, losing competitors with slaves. If he were to become a client freedman, would he have had any advantages over a well-treated slave? And anyway, a client dealt on his patron's behalf in public. How could a former runaway do this?

But as I wrote above, Paul had a much more ambitious plan than making Onesimus legally free. He wanted to make him into a human being, and he had a paradigm. As God chose and loved and guided the Israelites, he had now chosen and loved and could guide everyone. The grace of God could make what was subhuman into what was more than human. It was just a question of knowing it and letting it happen.

The way Paul makes the point in his letter to Philemon is beyond ingenious. He equates Onesimus with a son and a brother. He turns what Greco-Roman society saw as the fundamental, insurmountable differences between a slave and his master into an immense joke.

This chapter and previous ones have given some idea of who the most and the least replaceable people were in the eyes of the Greeks and Romans. I just want to stress again how crucial the relationship was between freeborn fathers and their legitimate sons, and between full freeborn brothers. Along with the misconstruing of ancient slavery, a huge barrier to modern readers' getting Philemon is that we can't, just from our own experience, see fatherhood and brotherhood as sacred—they have not been so for hundreds of years.

The Greeks and Romans had, until this time, not put

much stock in individual or spiritual immortality. Only in a tiny class were education and opportunity so good as to make talent a factor. And only around their edges did polytheistic religion and philosophy promise a better deal in the afterlife: most people didn't have access to such rituals and ideas. But all ordinary free people found ready in their families a chance to live on. (One of the greatest cruelties of slavery was that, having no legal family, a slave was boxed off in time, without a real tomb or recognized descendants or anything else to ensure he was remembered.) In the long run, the efforts of free people's lives served mainly the next generation, so of course this next generation had to exist: having children was vital. Men transmitted the clan names and most of the property and represented the family publicly, so the father-son relationship was the most important.

At both ends of epic poetry, early and Greek, and late and Roman, fathers and sons are glorified. In the *Iliad,* Hector in facing death on the battlefield in the name of honor has a single hope and ambition, that his son, Astyanax ("Lord of the City"), will be better regarded than he himself is:

He kissed his darling baby and caressed him
And sent Zeus and the other gods this prayer:
"Zeus and the other gods, let my child here
Also be great—like me—among the Trojans,
Outstanding, powerful, the lord of Ilium.
Let someone say: 'Much better than his father!'
As he comes back from war with bloodstained loot
From a dead enemy—to delight his mother."

In the *Aeneid,* Aeneas must push on and on past any romantic love or civil peace toward power—because of his son Iulus, who will carry on the dynasty. After a series of disasters and false starts, Aeneas has it very good in Carthage, with a royal girlfriend, Dido. But Hermes descends to shove him on his way, which will cause Dido's death:

He set his feathered feet among the shanties
And saw Aeneas laying out the towers
And building houses. Tawny jasper flecked
His sword. His shoulders trailed the glowing richness
Of a purple cloak with thin gold stripes, a present
Woven by wealthy Dido. The god scolded:
"Your wife must like you placing the foundations
For lofty Carthage, such a splendid city—
Forgetting your own kingdom that awaits you.
The ruler of the gods, whose strength bends heaven
And earth, has sent me down from bright Olympus,
Commanding that I fly here with this message:
What will this loitering in Libya bring you?
If you're unmoved by all the coming splendor,
Which is a weight you do not wish to shoulder,
Think of your hopes as Iulus grows, your heir,
Owed an Italian realm and Roman soil.

On this topic, I can let 'er rip. If you want one word to define social organization, religion, and values in general for the Greeks and Romans, you can't do better than "fatherhood." Zeus (for the Greeks) or Jupiter (for the Romans) was the father-god of the heavens, which made him king of creation. "The Father" and "the Begetter" are his common epithets. His power directed all the other gods, and his usual great intervention, besides in the weather, was in begetting:

heroes, young gods, legendary figures. He was the fountainhead of mythology and ritual.

He was also an excellent symbol of the neurotic extremes of paternal feeling among the mythmakers, in his creepy innovations in fertility that suggest an actual jealousy of the act of giving birth. He is "forced" by his own unthinking promise to incinerate his human lover Semele but somehow manages to snatch her unborn son Dionysus/Liber from her womb, sew him into his own thigh, and give birth to him at full term. His warlike daughter Athena/Minerva, with her masculine intelligence, was born from his head after he devoured her pregnant mother. It would be easy to dismiss these myths as garblings of prehistoric nightmares, were not their ideas so thoroughly borne out during the historical period. Euripides' tragic hero Hippolytus, for example, wants a means of obtaining children in which women have no part. Why can't men just buy them at temples, for example, getting better specimens the more they pay? A male fantasy common in the modern West is sex without fertility. A common ancient one was apparently fertility without sex.

The Romans went beyond the Greeks in deifying human fatherhood. A father's legal power over his child was absolute as long as they both lived. Legitimate children as a group in a household were termed the *liberi,* "the free ones," not because they could do as they liked, but only because they weren't slaves. Roman fathers could be indulgent in small things, but in the large ones they were the main force behind the iron regimen of conformity in their era: strict chastity for female children, military service for males, and pragmatically advantageous arranged marriages for both—just for a start. Fathers were also the main sources of opportunity: property, income, trades, professions, and social standing tended not to vary much from generation to generation but instead to flow straight through families. They flowed through fathers.

Brothers also played important roles in the Greek and Roman social systems. They were supposed to have close bonds of trust and affection, which were idealized in myth and history. The archetypal brothers were the gods Castor and Pollux. In one version of their story, the immortal brother refuses to accept the death of the mortal one and extracts from Zeus permission to sacrifice part of his own godhead so that the two can remain together: they now spend alternate days on Olympus and in the underworld. In another ending, they become a constellation, the Twins, or Gemini.

In Roman thinking, the legendary first king Romulus's killing of his brother, Remus, was almost like original sin, a presage of the heinous "fraternal slaughter" in the civil wars: Romans, people of the same blood, essentially of the same clan, tragically echoed Romulus's crime.

Since there was no rule of primogeniture (by which the eldest son gets most or all of the inheritance) among either the Greeks or the Romans, brothers were on a fairly equal footing and were expected to collaborate constantly for the good of the family. "Brother" could be a metaphor for other close and equal relationships, but Greeks and Romans never used the term to *create* a sense of closeness and equality out of division. Christians did, which at the start would have seemed bizarre. Imagine the impropriety of calling everybody at an open religious gathering "husbands and wives." In fact, a rumor that did much damage to the early church was that the meetings of "brothers and sisters" involved incest.

A deep, broad, menacing chasm cut slaves off from legitimate children and free blood siblings. A slave was a *filius neminis,* a son of no one. No man could claim him as a child, and no slave could make a claim on any man as his father. He could never be sure who his full biological siblings were—not that, officially, it mattered. But Paul unites all of these categories in writing of Onesimus, in the most thoroughgoing, absurd set of paradoxes in all of his letters:

1. Onesimus, though a slave, is Paul's son.
2. Onesimus, though an adult, has just been born.
3. Paul, though a prisoner, has begotten a son.
4. Paul, though physically helpless, is full of joy and confidence.
5. Paul is ecstatic to have begotten a runaway slave.
6. It is a sacrifice for Paul to send Onesimus back: he selfishly wants the services of this runaway slave for himself; conversely, he gives away his beloved newborn son.
7. Paul has wanted Onesimus to remain with him in place of Philemon, as if a runaway slave could be as much use to him, and in the same capacities, as the slave's master.
8. Onesimus's flight must result not in punishment but in promotion to brotherhood with his master.
9. Onesimus ("Profitable") was perhaps unprofitable when treated as a slave and certainly unprofitable as a runaway, but will be profitable when treated as a beloved brother.
10. Onesimus will be profitable not only to his master but even to Paul.
11. Onesimus, a runaway slave, must be treated as having the same value as Paul himself.

12. Paul promises emphatically to pay any monetary damages, but Philemon will (the reader senses) not take him up on this.
13. Philemon will acknowledge and act on all of this of his own free will, not needing any direct command or explanation from Paul for this rather devastating-looking set of policies.
14. Paul is confident that Philemon will do even more than he asks, but what is he asking? For Philemon to make Onesimus his brother in practical terms is impossible; even if Philemon took the dizzying step of making him an heir, he could not share with him his own privileges as a freeborn person (assuming he is one)—laws forbid it. But even as a figure of speech or an ideal, what does "brother" mean? It is as if Paul were writing, "I'm thinking of a big, *big* number. Guess what it is!"

Paul may also be parodying letters of recommendation.* Such letters of Cicero have a similar fulsomeness, and a similar confident self-mockery as does the letter to Philemon. A common come-on is along the lines of "I'm ridiculously excited about this person, but of course you'll indulge me because of the valuable relationship between ourselves." Cicero, like Paul, takes the whole responsibility and promises wonderful benefits. But Cicero's letters of recommendation either ask for specific things or are about people who will ably figure out on their own what to do with a new connection. And Cicero always stresses the personal merits of the subject:

*He plays explicitly on the idea of "Letters of recommendation" in 2 Corinthians 3:1.

> But if because of his shyness he hasn't put himself in your way, or if you're not yet well enough acquainted with him, or if there's any reason that he needs a greater endorsement, I hereby recommend him to such a great degree that I couldn't praise anyone else more eagerly or for better reasons. And I'll do what people do who write these letters conscientiously and with no ulterior motives. I'll promise you, or rather I'll pledge in the fullest and most binding terms to you, that Manius Curtius is such a good person, and such a humane one, that if you get to know him, you'll think him worth it, and worth such a fancy recommendation.

Imagine, in this tradition, a prisoner writing on behalf of a runaway slave and perhaps a thief, who may have no personal merits whatsoever or may just now be starting to show some, and who could not normally find hope in anything but pleas for mercy on his behalf from a man of material power and influence with whom he has taken shelter. "Comic inversion" just doesn't cover what is going on in this letter. In worldly terms, it is like a janitor throwing a party for his dog and inviting a federal judge.

The solution, the punch line of the joke that is the letter to Philemon, the climax of this farce, is God. God alone has the power to make a runaway slave a son and brother, and in fact to make any mess work out for the good—not that anyone knows how, but it doesn't matter. Philemon has only to surrender to the grace, peace, love, and faith the letter urges, and the miracle will happen. Paul seems to insist that it is happening even as he prays for it, and he is goofy with joy: Philemon cannot say no to him, because God cannot say no.

This unusual experience of prayer drives Paul to new

heights (a strange but, I think, appropriate term) of self-deprecation. More here than anywhere else, he makes fun of his own weaknesses. He is often in his letters the nagging father, using metaphors of birth and rearing infants, boasting of his sacrifices, losing his temper, prodding, repeating, condescending—doing so many things to suggest that the outcome depends on him, not God.

At first glance, he appears to do the same sort of thing here. He twists Philemon's arm by stressing his own pathetic situation and Philemon's spiritual debt to him, and by citing devoted followers (some of whom may be Philemon's friends). But he leaves Philemon without a to-do list, and with only (only?) an assurance of profound love and purpose. He turns his sermonizing into a bomb, presses down the detonator, and walks away, leaving glittering fragments of absurdity in place of the conviction that people solve problems.

This could be called a cop-out, a pie in the sky. But in the most practical terms, he was justified: the early Christian church, without staging any actual campaign against slavery, in the course of the centuries weakened it until it all but disappeared from Europe. Slavery was doomed simply because it jarred with Christian feeling—the same basic circumstance that doomed it in the modern West. But Paul is not calculating anything of the kind. He is simply turning in Onesimus—and Philemon, and himself, and the whole community—to God.

So it's no wonder that there's been such resistance to dealing with this letter on its own terms, instead of substituting some congenial mundane opinion or interest for the dizzying submission to God that it shows.

Picture me standing in a South African shack settlement,

or what used to be one. Somebody knocked over a kerosene lamp, and there is sand and ash and melted plastic where the shacks used to be. I've come out with a Council of Churches donation of clothes and food. A local minister speaks to the crowd for a few minutes in Xhosa, and adds a prayer.

But now a chubby man in a beautiful suit has stepped up to the microphone. He has on a frilly green and yellow badge like a prom corsage. He is the representative of the country's ruling party, the African National Congress. He speaks in Xhosa for twenty minutes. He gestures toward the emergency shelters, the army tents that my tax dollars paid for, and then at his own chest.

There isn't any worship or other gathering you can keep these people away from. If they've done nothing at all, they still demand a cut of the publicity. I'm going to get the Council of Churches to pass a resolution to at least keep the sons of bitches out of pulpits.

Today, back in the States, I can't tell whose rightness and righteousness was uglier, theirs of the victory over apartheid, or mine of white charity in triumphal procession. But I read Philemon and see that there is only one way to win.

CHAPTER 7: LOVE JUST IS: PAUL ON THE FOUNDATION OF THE NEW COMMUNITY

When I read 1 Corinthians 13 for the first time in the original Greek, I understood better why I had always felt shut out and bored during the reading of the passage at a wedding. I had misunderstood. Love is not some special dispensation, some perfect, abiding state of harmony for the lucky, as if those who can perform up to Paul's stated standard will get the same performance granted to them forever, and as if those who can't will lose their place in the community, will not have friends or lovers or spouses or children or a God. Love is something that is there already, something that draws the mind and heart back to itself.

I first got a hint of this when I looked at the comparatively obscure runup to the famous passage. In 1 Corinthians 12, Paul has been writing of the church as one body with many parts. Jews and Greeks, slaves and the free all partake of this unity. These people have many different talents and need one another the way an eye needs a hand. They are all incomplete, and they must all cooperate for that very reason.

"Are all apostles? Are all prophets? Are all teachers? Do all work miracles? Do all possess gifts for healing? Do all speak in tongues? Do all interpret?" (12:29–30). The lecture is showing typical irritability.

But then Paul seems to catch himself and turn back (12:31–13:1), as if he realizes that he is acting out incompleteness, an incompleteness of a more basic kind. He might as well be writing, "Do all have patience? Are all gentle with people who are trying to find their way? Do all admit that they don't know everything? *I* have failed in the most fundamental things."

> 31 But strive for the greater gifts. And I will show
> you a still more excellent way.
> 13 If I speak in the tongues of mortals and of
> angels, but do not have love, I am a noisy gong
> or a clanging cymbal. 2 And if I have prophetic pow-
> ers, and understand all mysteries and all knowledge,
> and if I have all faith, so as to remove mountains, but
> do not have love, I am nothing. 3 If I give away all my
> possessions, and if I hand over my body so that I may
> boast, but do not have love, I gain nothing.

Let me first back up and make sure that Paul's topic is explicit. As I noted in chapter 2, in Greek there was *erōs* for sexual desire and being "in love"; *philia* for the affection of family and friends; and *agapē,* a marginal word adapted to carry the central message of Christianity. *Agapē* is selfless love that people can feel even for enemies or strangers. It is utterly impractical and makes no sense, but it is real. It comes from God. *Agapē* is 1 Corinthians 13 love.

Though he had a word to use that at least couldn't be mistaken for lust, Paul still doesn't seem to be confident of getting his point across to his readers in Corinth. And no wonder: he is writing about an utterly new idea. Among the polytheists, giving always fit into some rationale: open-handed hospitality, which made trade and travel mutually safer; self-sacrifice in war, which helped create military machines; the love of children or parents that bound households together; and male friendships that were the basis of politics and business. Practice love for its own sake? Huh?

Paul, in starting to explain *agapē,* is facing the goal of his life and his mission, and he is facing it from a highly personal angle. He has shifted from the third person to the first. If he was showing no humility before, he is showing it now. He, the leader, the apostle, the preacher, is worthless in all of his achievements if he does not have love. His words here take apart not the polytheistic culture but, blessing by blessing, his own church under his own guidance.

Does anyone else hear a hint of real exasperation with himself as he starts out, as if he is taking himself down an extra peg with the expression "of mortals and of angels"? It sounds to me a little like someone saying, "I might speak as well as a person could speak; I might speak as well as the queen of England."

English-speaking Christians, unless they've been brought up with updated translations, come to the first sentence with a handicap, the image of "tongues." Before I saw the Greek, it never really registered with me that these were not body parts but languages: the same word serves for both, but "language" is the logical translation here.

Paul is referring to glossolalia, or "speaking in tongues." This was a unique, charter practice of Christians, a token of the birth of the church at Pentecost. The gift of tongues signaled that the new faith was for everyone, cosmopolitan or not, and that God would speak to them and through them in their own languages.

But look at how Paul characterizes speaking in tongues without "love"—without true self-sacrifice. In his metaphor for empty sound, one of the verbs is the proper one for metal ringing, but the other is usually about a human voice, in a war or victory shout or mourning—or, especially, a shriek during the wild rituals of Bacchus, the wine god, rituals brought to Greece from the East within legendary memory and to Rome within the time of recorded history.

The nouns are literally "brass" (or "bronze") and "cymbal"; the rhetorical figure is a hendiadys, or "one through two": it is a brass or bronze cymbal we are reading about. This image was used for bombast or self-advertisement: the on-the-make provincial writer Apion (whose life overlapped with Paul's) was styled "the world's cymbal." But at this period, this object had its strongest link with ecstatic celebration in mystery cults, particularly that of Cybele and other Asian mother goddesses whose identity and ritual, in popular opinion when not in reality, were interchangeable.

Of all the cults Paul could have alluded to, those of Bacchus and Cybele were the most noxious in the popular mind. Their original foreignness made them suspect in the first place, and people associated them with orgies and crimes. Here is Livy's account of the cult of Bacchus in Rome before it was banned. (See also p. 64 about this episode.)

> When wine, smutty talk, night, and the mingling of the sexes had snuffed out any notion of restraint, then

> perversions of every kind began to go forward, as everybody found ready that sort of pleasure to which he or she was individually and naturally inclined. And the abandonment wasn't limited to sex between freeborn men and women; no, this warehouse of crime sent out perjury, counterfeiting, and entire false prosecutions, as well as poisonings and assassinations so discreet and professional that in certain cases the families could not even find the bodies for burial. Conspiracy produced some of the crimes, but most were simply violent; because of the shrieking and the noise of drums and cymbals, no one outside heard the cries of those being manhandled or killed.

Cybele's cult evoked the ancient horror of passive homosexuality and effeminacy (see chapter 3). Some of her followers were men who had castrated themselves in the transports of dancing rites. Lucretius uses Cybele's worship as a warning example of religious overexcitement. Vergil in the *Aeneid* shows the Italians of a millennium before taunting the settlers from Troy with their "effeminate" Asian culture and sneering at the Great Mother and her rites. Juvenal ranked this cult among the exploitative ones in Rome, a couple of generations after Paul's death. A naïve woman is a natural victim:

Here comes the troupe
Of raving Bellona, the gods' mother. The junior pervert
Must worship the giant eunuch like an icon,
Who grabbed a shard and cut his tender balls off
Long ago. The loud crew, the lowly players

Of drums fall back before his droopy headdress
From Phrygia. He blares a threat: September's south wind
Will bring disease should she not cleanse herself
With a hundred eggs, and second-hand red robes—
For him.

A couple of generations later, Apuleius depicted the cult as the worst kind of scam, one that played on simple people's superstition and compassion.

> When they came to the outside gate, they immediately flew forward with frantic-sounding, discordant howls. They put their heads down and for a long time whipped their necks around slickly and whirled their loose long hair. Now and then they attacked their own flesh with their teeth, and at last they each took the double-edged swords they carried and cut up their own arms.
>
> Amidst all of this, one of them went more lavishly wild and, panting rapidly from deep in his lungs as if full of divine inspiration, he faked a visitation of madness—as if the presence of the gods didn't make men better but instead broke them down and filled them with disease. . . .
>
> With a phony, shrieking show of channeling some holy message, he launched an accusation against himself, saying that he had committed some sin against the sanctity of cultic observance; and he demanded just punishment for his crime from his own hand. Grabbing the whip that is the essential accessory of these faggots—twisted ribbons of unshaven sheepskin

> bordered at intervals with a lot of sheep jointbones—
> he kept thrashing himself with its multiknotted blows.

These performances are for shaking down audiences, but the group stops at nothing, not even at the passive gang rape of an innocent young man. And when the narrator, a man turned into a donkey, first falls into their hands, the slave they have been passively abusing gives soulful thanks that he will get a break now, as his masters will of course turn their sexual attentions to this animal.

And the authors of these grim scenes were polytheists, used to cruel gods who brought disaster or death at whim, and used to coughing up to greedy priests for any hope of divine help. Cybele and Bacchus obviously had cults quite out of the ordinary. There has to be a special noxious flavor to Paul's allusions to them. Christians who depend on noisy shows, in no matter how Christian a category, are no better than polytheists at their most abandoned and cynical.

Next, Paul cites "prophetic powers" (literally "prophecy"). For the polytheists, prophecy was the interpretation of the gods' will, especially through commercial oracles. For the Christians, prophecy was the public voicing of inspired and inspirational things about the new faith. Contempt for polytheist practice is probably present here in Paul—since this is a shared word—but the Christian "gift" he criticizes when it lacks love is otherwise a commendable one, not ever merely puzzling to others, as speaking in tongues can be. Paul praises prophecy over speaking in tongues from the start of 1 Corinthians 14. In harshly qualifying its value here, he is moving closer to the heart of the problem: nothing people do is worthwhile unless they love one another.

"Mysteries" were not a vague category of unknowable things for the Greeks and Romans, but a definite set of secret rites—"mysterious" because even the initiates had to shut their eyes at certain stages: the root word is "to shut one's eyes." Mysteries for Christians were divine truth revealed by grace. A similar idea comes across in Paul's mention of "knowledge," which in Greek and Roman literature could be about actually knowing ultimate truths through supreme human skill. In early Christianity the word "knowledge" carried the notion that any grasp of such truths was a divine favor, a loving support of trust-filled, admitted human weakness.

To sum up, glossolalia, through the image of the shriek and the gong, as well as prophecy, mysteries, and knowledge, just by shared terms, evokes uncomfortable comparisons to polytheist practice. The idea must be "You *are* like them if you don't have love."

Now, as if to pound in that selfish behavior is a challenge Christians have to own up to within their own unique community, Paul shifts away from words that have anything to do with polytheistic religion or philosophy. *Pistis,* the next word—"faith" (which I discussed on pp. 38–39)—had a very special religious meaning for Christians, and "removing mountains" has the obvious reference to Jesus' promise (Matthew 21:21; Mark 11:23). We have now moved wholly into Christian territory. In the phrase "give away all my possessions," the Greek verb is not actually "give away" but "feed by hand." The reference is to charity in Jewish and Christian practice. The polytheists had beggars among them, but I don't read anywhere of a religious duty to care for such people unless they were attached to a particular cult (which, as in the case of the Great Mother, might just be a shakedown of the superstitious), and giving away everything to them would have been considered merely insane.

A textual problem arises in verse 3, but I think that modern editors have solved it. Handing over the body "to be burned" is what the King James and closely related translations have, but nobody was burning martyrs at this point, as far as we know. "So that I may boast," from the Greek verb that is attested in some manuscripts, makes a lot more sense.

Giving up possessions and life—there had been people contributing all of their property to Christian fellowships, and there had been martyrs already, such as Stephen—would seem to be pretty acceptable expressions of love, unless these things are done just to show off, in the same spirit as staging a noisy ceremony, shooting off one's mouth, or pulling off miracles as if they were magic tricks. "Boast" ties the phrase straight to Paul: he is always boasting; he even makes fun of himself boasting (2 Corinthians 11).

Imagine how this catalog put readers on the spot. If they thought that their Christian activities—however enthusiastic or seemingly successful—would save them, they were wrong, in an embarrassingly polytheistic way. Jesus had spoken similarly about *agapē* (as the gospel writers render his Aramaic word): non-Jews manage to love their friends; there is nothing special about you unless you surrender to a much more significant love (Matthew 5:43–47).

But I feel less moved by that than I do by the thought of the apostle's forgetting love altogether and then suddenly, at just the right moment, remembering it in its importance beyond anything. How could this happen, unless God could keep love, guard it for a person until he and everyone else is ready? This would seem to be an absurd degree of grace—

unless Paul carries here again his frequent point that there *are* no limits.

WHAT IS *agapē,* then? Paul begins to answer this, with several sharp shifts in focus.

> 4 Love is patient; love is kind; love is not envious or
> boastful or arrogant 5 or rude. It does not insist on its
> own way; it is not irritable or resentful; 6 it does not
> rejoice in wrongdoing, but rejoices in the truth. 7 It
> bears all things, believes all things, hopes all things,
> endures all things.
>
> 8 Love never ends. But as for prophecies, they will
> come to an end; as for tongues, they will cease; as for
> knowledge, it will come to an end.

Paul has been speaking in the first person, but now moves to the third. Love is something outside himself, but really more like a someone, since it does so many things and has so many human characteristics. Before, we were reading of religion, but most of the way through this present list, we find nothing that can apply directly to a relationship with God, only to relationships with other human beings—unless we can somehow imagine that God needs kindness or patience. Only at the end do more-religious words come back: rejoicing in the truth, believing, hoping. But the repeated "all things" (or "everything") in verse 7 suggests that the goal is still to deal with the everyday world in an exemplary way. These humble virtues are what absolutely never come to an end. They outlast any worship, wisdom, or inspiration.

The break in style in the Greek at the beginning of this section is startling. I made a long search for parallels to this new style, and I ended up feeling like a pedantic moron for missing the point: these words are not *supposed* to be like anything else.

It's more or less a necessity of our language that the standard translations here contain a lot of adjectives. The Greek does not contain a single one. Instead we have a mass of verbs, things love does and doesn't do. This is the ultimate authority for the saying "Love is a verb."

Since the wording is so simple, I can translate this piece fairly literally without creating nonsense. I am also going to take out spaces between the words, punctuation, and the distinction between capital and small letters—none of these would have appeared in the original ancient manuscript. Below is an English version of what Paul's readers saw on the page. To get a sense of what it sounded like when read aloud (a very common practice everywhere, but doubtless more common in the Christian churches, where many members were illiterate), read three times as fast as you would normally, in the typical manner of a Mediterranean language. This will produce something closer to the original machine gun of verbs:

> THELOVEENDURESLONGACTSKINDLYTHE
> LOVENOTACTSJEALOUSLYNOTACTSBRUTALLY
> NOTBOASTSNOTGETSFULLOFITSELFNOT
> DISGRACESITSELFNOTSEEKSWHATISITS
> OWNNOTGETSIRRITATEDNOTRECKONS
> UPTHEEVILNOTREJOICESINTHEINJUSTICE
> BUTREJOICESTOGETHERINTHETRUTH
> ENDURESEVERYTHINGBELIEVESEVERYTHING
> HOPESEVERYTHINGENDURESEVERYTHING
> THELOVENEVERFALLS

So manically verb-centered is the passage that Paul takes two adjectives and creates a one-word verb from each (neither verb being attested previously in Greek); and he creates yet another verb, in Greek a one-word metaphor:

1. "[is] kind" (verb: "kinds")
2. "[is] boastful" (verb: "boastfuls")
3. "[is] arrogant" (verb: "inflates-like-a-bellows")

If we take the meaning from the form, we could say that he is preaching, "You know the right ways to feel? Turn those feelings into *acts* and perform those acts, ceaselessly. You know the wrong ways to feel? Don't, ever, perform the acts that spring from them."

Love is not just something to return to. It is something to remember to do. And are Paul's followers ever in for a challenge here. To love everyone selflessly is a lot harder than to sober up, stop fighting, and behave decently, or to bring justice to the weak, or to accommodate a spouse, or to deeply respect authority, or even to be open to whatever status in life God's purpose and providence may grant. How could anyone manage to follow 1 Corinthians 13 and not go insane?

It might be possible if love is not an ethereal, abstract standard, an impossible assignment written in lightning on a rock, but a living God. Suppose the love people need to carry out loves them and helps them, sometimes through the other people it loves, and sometimes merely as itself. Suppose it reaches out, calls, never gives up on failure. Suppose that, though human beings fail most of the time, love never does.

. . .

IF THE LOVE that attends humans comes from a perfect sacrifice of a perfect being, anything they can give has to be petty and confused in comparison.

> 9 For we know only in part, and we prophesy only
> in part; 10 but when the complete comes, the partial
> will come to an end. 11 When I was a child, I spoke
> like a child, I thought like a child, I reasoned like a
> child; when I became an adult, I put an end to childish
> ways. 12 For now we see in a mirror, dimly, but then
> we will see face to face. Now I know only in part; then
> I will know fully, even as I have been fully known. 13
> And now faith, hope, and love abide, these three; and
> the greatest of these is love.

What could be less coherent and satisfying than Paul's earthly life? He disappeared for long periods after his conversion, three years in Arabia and a number of years back home in Tarsus. He may have worked in his family business, argued with his parents, married and argued with his wife. He then helped with the new movement in Antioch, and later in a long series of other cities. He pitched and vomited on boats. He was shipwrecked three times, and once floated a whole day and night on wreckage. Time after time, he lay awake hungry and cold in long grass by the road, perhaps listening terrified as bandits passed.

Sometimes after he preached, they whipped him until his back was a single wound, and in town after town they beat him with rods, but he wouldn't shut up. He had an uncanny gift, not only for inspiring and convincing, but also for causing riots. And with a pen that must have eaten through the papyrus like acid, he cursed his rival missionaries and made fun of his converts. He even quarreled with the gentle, widely respected Barnabas, who had sponsored him and looked after him, making a missionary out of him in spite of everything that told the others he was trouble.

He sat and stitched together pieces of leather tents with an awl to support himself and earn boat fare; there were easier ways for an educated man to make money, but they required cooperation, and in that sense he was probably unemployable. He found some sympathetic people and started small congregations, but he seems to have been congenitally unable to share authority. He even fell out with Peter and spread the word that he was a hypocrite. Paul was just not a nice guy. He even had his half-Jewish assistant Timothy circumcised as an adult. Rescued a final time from a mob, he parlayed Roman protective custody into a trip to Rome. In the midst of everything, he wrote 1 Corinthians 13.

It would all have been nothing but a long and useless farce if not for its faith and its passion. His stumbling, incomplete self yearned toward completeness. He sums this up in the insistent image of himself as a child.

I spent a long time trying to understand my feelings about this image. I had found it uncomfortably moving even when I was a child, but for some reason its strangeness and power only increased as I grew. It was the only part of the passage I liked, but it was . . . I didn't know. I believe now that from the time I was used to anything in the Bible, I *wasn't* used to people in it talking about themselves as children, the way people tirelessly do in modern literature.

Childhood certainly plays a special role in Christianity. Christ was a baby at first, and children in their innocence and weakness are supposed to have a special bond with and special protection from Christ. But of small children's own points of view we have practically nothing in the Bible. We hear the words of Jesus at the age of twelve, but they are superadult words inspired out of another world, putting his anxious parents in their place (Luke 2:49).

My years as a student of the classics must have confirmed my impression that in those days, children more or less weren't there—an impression that fits with what we know of most traditional cultures: until they are initiated (usually at puberty), the young are sort of half human, with no firm stake in the community.

I made a list of Greek and Roman literary treatments of actual personality in childhood, and a pretty short list it was. On it was the Homeric Hymn to Hermes (unknown date, but probably fifth century B.C. or later—or else earlier but badly corrupted by later writers), in which a god rustles cattle, hoodwinks a divine tribunal, makes three major inventions, and receives authority over a cult, all within a few hours after he is born. The same kind of comical precocity is found in stories about the love god Eros (in the Greek world) or Cupid (in the Roman one). The pounding irony is that this toddler has power over the strongest, proudest adults and even over other gods. In Apollonius Rhodius's epic the *Argonautica* (third century B.C.), his divine mother Aphrodite discovers the boy busy at the equivalent of card counting, taking another young god for everything he has. In Apuleius, Cupid French-kisses his mother (Venus, in this Roman tale) before leaving with his bow and arrows on an assignment.

All right, those are gods, so I couldn't expect realistic depictions. But human childhood as seen through ancient books isn't believable either. Even in writing tenderly of his own two-year-old's death, Plutarch specifies among her merits only implausible precocity in kindness and generosity: his daughter (according to him) offered to share her wet nurse's milk with her toys and with other children ("as if inviting them to dinner"). The poet Callimachus, in his prologue to the *Aetia (Causes),* shows his early self as another superhuman child, taking a tablet onto his knees not to learn to write but to pour forth epic poetry. He is mistaken only about the genre: his true calling, as a god instantly informs him, is to pen incredibly learned, precious, short poems. Various leaders manifested their greatness or their depravity in early childhood, according to late biographies, but that's a lot of hoo-ha.

It is probably safe to state that ancient Greek and Roman authors never write realistically of themselves as children. One fictional character speaking honestly of himself as a child (as well as playing indulgently with a child, as I show on pp. 56–58) is the drunken, gauche freedman Trimalchio in Petronius. He reveals that he used to be a slave catamite and voices a child's pathetic justification: "It's not wrong if the master makes you do it." Since that kind of vulnerability, if not that kind of abuse, just went along with immaturity for the Greeks and Romans, it is natural that they shrank from exposing their immaturity, even through memory.

Realizing all of this confirmed why Paul's "When I was a child . . ." is odd. He even refers to himself as a *nēpios.* He cannot mean this in the Classical Greek sense—that kind of *nēpios* was a baby who could not speak yet, and the little Paul can speak, think, and reason to some extent. But he is still a young child, with a realistically limited outlook. The words must have come across to contemporaries as a shattering way for Paul to illustrate the incompleteness, the unconsciousness of all mortals. Because only the great gulf, in the eyes of the ancients, between a child and an adult can show the difference between people on their own and people unified with God, Paul makes a sacrifice of his dignity and his status as a man (here *anēr,* "man's man") and leader and creates an image of himself as a groping, hapless small percentage of a man. Now that's love.

The NRSV has it that we now see only "in a mirror, dimly"; literally, this is "through/by means of a mirror, in a riddle." The correction from the old translation "glass" (old-fashioned English for "mirror"), which is confusing to the modern ear, is good: I used to picture a dirty pane of window glass myself, whereas ancient mirrors were made not of glass but of bronze. Bronze does not reflect terribly well; people don't, on their own, in their immaturity, see even themselves clearly. But if they practice love, they will someday look into a mirror and see not only themselves but God. They will have the answer to the riddle and understand.

I picture Paul settling into a house in Rome, the last place he will live. He is arranging his room, putting his tent-making tools and a few spare clothes into a chest. He has some papyrus rolls of Jewish scripture, which he places in the slots of the bookcase. He is exhausted and starving, and his back is giving him trouble; he'll never be rid of the effects of so many beatings. He is starting to feel sorry for himself. He sighs, kneels down, and thanks God for arriving safely, and for all he can do here. This reminds him: why aren't the local Jewish leaders here already to talk to him?

I think nowadays that reading the epistles is better for me than reading the gospels. What can I understand about the way Jesus felt? But I *feel* how Paul must have felt.

The Stoics pictured two parallel lines, each starting from its own finite point and moving infinitely in the same direction, say left. But one line starts to the left of the other, so the one "infinity" is shorter. It's a paradox: true, demonstrable, yet incomprehensible. My sin feels infinite, but the love of God is infinite both within me and outside me, going in every imaginable direction, like the light of the sun compared to the beam of a laser pointer with which I play with the cat. I sit on the edge of the bed and grouse and daydream, but eventually I get up and go where I am called.

NOTE ON MY USE OF SOURCES

This is a new kind of book, I know. I worked in some new ways that I need to give an account of. My colleagues both in classics and in New Testament studies may ask, "What does she think she's doing?" Other readers may ask, "Is this what biblical scholarship at universities is like? Can she *do* this?" The answer to both groups is that, to make ancient voices better heard, I had to think more as a reader and a writer than as a traditional researcher.

This is why I brought in personal experiences and imaginative impressions in dealing with the texts. But I would never claim the right to be touchy-feely about these vital historical documents. On the contrary, I feel justified in writing reflectively about them only because I have lived with them for thirty years: learned their languages, studied their contexts, and made myself comfortable with their styles. When you know writers that well, you can have a sort of conversation with them, and if you go on and on about yourself or interrupt or contradict them, they will tell you, in your heart and conscience, that you are full of it.

My inquiries are directed almost entirely at the Greeks and Romans, with very limited treatment of the Jewish tradition in itself. But I did not look at the Greeks and Romans as entirely separate from the Jews and risk being lured into the tired and rather unfruitful debate over who had the greater influence on Paul. I didn't want or need to go there. Greco-Roman culture tended to assimilate conquered peoples with the force of a John Deere harvester, and at this period many Jews of the Diaspora lived and thought like Greeks and Romans most of the time (though Palestinian Jews formed the most stubborn resistance to Roman rule). Many Jews could not read Hebrew or Aramaic but had access to their own scriptures only in the Greek version, the Septuagint. When Paul used metaphors for sacred athletic games, which were alien to traditional Jewish culture, he was writing of something known everywhere in the empire through its main languages and literature—even as Pacific islanders today know about skiing through American media.

But things were quite complicated. Some Greeks and Romans were attached to Diaspora Jewish congregations from pre-Christian times, forming a special class of "God-fearers" or "God-worshippers"; these would have embraced quite a lot in the Jewish worldview. And Paul's Greek, drawing on the Septuagint as it often does, would have brought up many Jewish ideas and images in the minds of both God-fearers and Jews. The majority in the following generations of Christian converts, however, the great waves of the evangelized, started out thoroughly polytheistic. Polytheistic literature is an unequivocally good template for what the letters meant to them.

Anyway, to try to show on whose behalf or under whose influence Paul wrote in each instance is excessively challenging. It is also a project Paul himself would not have liked. I preferred to look at him from a point of view, the Greco-Roman one, that was the dominant one at the time, shared by vast populations to varying degrees and known today through exhaustively researched literature. But I want to stress that I am not disrespectful of Paul's Jewish context, which was vital—Paul was a proud Jew and cherished the origin of Christianity in Judaism. That context simply isn't my topic in this book.

In case I seem to be playing fast and loose with chronology by citing material written hundreds of years before the New Testament, I hope to justify myself in three ways. One is that Greco-Roman culture, clear into the imperial period and until Christianity itself began to change it fundamentally, was quite static compared with our culture. Parties in the evening, for example, were roughly the same for centuries. The second justification is the scarcity of some material. For instance, we haven't got an ancient Greek forensic speech on caught-in-the-act adultery newer than the late fifth or early fourth century B.C.—or any other Greek document of any period that tells us nearly as much about such adultery as the old one does. I cite the best of what is there. The third justification is that some of these texts were classics already, read and recited and included in school curricula down the generations; if they did not reflect lasting values (even when some customs and institutions had fallen away), their endurance would be hard to explain.

Readers will quickly notice that a number of the works I cite are bawdy and comic. I arrived at the study of the New Testament with the same interest in daily life that had brought me first to the Roman novelist Petronius and then to the Greek comedian Aristophanes. I want to know what was really on people's minds and in their lunch boxes. As far as Greco-Roman literature goes, scholars have tended to cite Plato, Seneca, and other philosophers in connection with Paul, alleging that he got certain ideas from them. If that were true, it would still leave a lot unsaid about what Paul faced and what his mission sought to change. He himself rejected intellectualizing (most explicitly at 1 Corinthians 1:18–25; "wisdom" is the common Bible translation, but the evidence is huge that ordinary people used the Greek word to mean "self-promoting, fact-twisting blather") and addressed himself to the practical problems of his churches, and to revealed religious truths far beyond human understanding. My expertise—the literature of food, clothes, sex, family squabbles, petty commerce, local politics, and staying out of the rain—is a better background to him, I believe, though I do cite from the entire range of Greco-Roman literature (including philosophy).

Expert readers might object that most of the literature I cite is quite sophisticated, even when it is obscene and treats lowlife. That is true; the Greeks and Romans handed down toilet humor and spoofs of their slaves in ornate literary forms. Much of Paul's audience would not have known this literature at first hand, though much of it claimed to be about them. So how relevant is it? In using it, as in using books from a very wide span of time, I can again call on justifications of necessity and common sense. Elite works are almost all we have of Greece's and Rome's literature, and they were dominant to a degree our elite works are not. These societies were steeply hierarchical, and in them the canon (the Roman one laid out by the master teacher Quintilian combined Greek and Latin literature) showed values that the lower classes both were strictly subject to and fervently dreamed of wielding—that is, until Christianity began to change minds. Any child formally schooled would learn at least some poetry (all of it written for adults, and uncensored), oratory (much of it full of dirt and slander), and history (violent): these were in fact the basic curriculum, for the powerful reason that they more or less diagrammed the society. They weren't a precise overlay of the experience of Paul's followers, but we have nothing better—not by far.

I have used mainly the obvious tools, such as Greek and Latin dictionaries and biblical and classical commentaries, besides the original texts.

For a Greek text of the New Testament, I had no hesitation in choosing the Nestlē-Aland edition. Its authority is unrivaled, and its format is accessible to a scholar like myself, who has been trained but never professionally active in "textual criticism"; this is the art and science of reconstructing the likely authentic text of a work of ancient literature after that work has been transmitted through a long series of cumulatively corrupt handwritten copies. The state of the Greek text explains some of the main confusions about Paul, so that I needed to go into certain text-critical questions. But I have kept these forays as brief and straightforward as possible, nearly always relying on the consensus represented in Nestlē-Aland rather than indulging in speculation of my own. This stuff is fascinating to me—but not to many others, I think.

I have made quite limited use of "secondary literature" such as scholarly monographs and journal articles, except as examples of how badly Paul can be misunderstood. Two observations confirmed that this was a good choice. First, it was clear that in biblical studies, as in classics, really valuable information and insights would soon enough find their way into that special and privileged class of secondary literature, the reference books that I mentioned above: I didn't have to—in essence—compile my own versions of them.

Secondly, I found no great difference between the persuasiveness of typical modern academic writing on the Bible and of older writing on the Bible that was openly political or theological, making no claim to objective research or evaluation. Yet to yield to my impulses and spend a lot of time on criticism of secondary sources in either class would have been to take my eyes off Paul, to place my own opinions at the center of this book. I wanted above all to avoid that, and to offer an account of the apostle that will last longer and be more valuable than anything I could write on my own behalf, as a competing scholar and nothing else.

The translation of the Bible I quote is the New Revised Standard Version, except in chapter 2, with its passage from the King James.

It took me a long time to decide on this; I considered doing some of my own translation, because I sometimes disagreed with everything else available for a word or sentence. I thought of using only the King James Bible, because of its familiarity and influence. I wondered about making a broad selection of translations. But in the end I felt that the NRSV was the best because of the vast, up-to-date scholarship behind it and at the same time its retention of a lot of traditional wording. With generous notes and appendices balancing out this wording, as in the *New Oxford Annotated Bible* (the edition that I referred to the most), I could best see the tradition in development, the Bibles of my childhood moving at a stately pace into the future.

The NRSV is updated but doesn't have more political correctness than the Greek can support. For example, the old generalizing "man," which the NRSV eschews, is *linguistically* insensitive, not just vulnerable to charges of sexism: the original Greek word is grammatically masculine but means only "person" or "human being." (In fact, the word can be grammatically feminine and mean "prostitute" in the sense of "that *person* whom I am too polite to specify as a prostitute.") There is a separate word for persons whose male anatomy and masculine character are important.

But in chapter 2, which responds to a Puritan minister's use of Paul, I felt I could quote only the King James, the Bible the minister knew, particularly because its tone (and even the version of the original Greek text it was based on) supported a certain kind of interpretation. The NRSV would not show as clearly where Richard Baxter was coming from. Where I don't agree with translations in the NRSV or the King James or other Bibles, I have of course said so.

The translations of Greco-Roman texts are all my own. They are as close to the originals as I could bring them, though some may seem strikingly slangy or ironic, unlike other translations of classical literature. I made it a point to try to catch the original tones and registers, as far as English idiom allows. (I had to let most of the formal structures go, however: the original meters, prose rhythms, and so on are simply too alien and too complicated. I have rendered the more brutal erotic poetry as plain prose, unless I had a verse translation already on hand in one of my published books.) I have made words or phrases stand out only after my research convinced me that they stood out for the original readers or audiences.

SELECTED BIBLIOGRAPHY

Adam, Adela Marion, editor. *Plato: The Apology of Socrates.* Cambridge: Cambridge University Press, 1914.

Anthon, Charles, editor. *The Anabasis of Xenophon.* New York: Harper and Brothers, 1870.

Arbesmann, Rudolph, O.S.A., Sister Emily Joseph Daly, C.S.J., and Edwin A. Quain, S.J., translators. *Tertullian: Apologetical Works and Minucius Felix: Octavius.* New York: Fathers of the Church, Inc., 1950.

Armstrong, Karen. *Through the Narrow Gate.* New York: St. Martin's Press, 1981.

Bailey, Cyril, editor and translator. *Titi Lucreti Cari De Rerum Natura Libri Sex.* Oxford: Clarendon Press, 1947.

Bailey, D. R. Shackleton, editor. *Q Horati Flacci Opera.* Stuttgart: Teubner, 1985.

Barber, E. A., editor. *Sexti Properti Carmina,* 2nd ed. Oxford: Oxford University Press, 1960.

Barth, Karl. *The Epistle to the Romans,* translated from the 6th ed. by Edwyn C. Hoskyns. London: Oxford University Press, 1933.

Barth, Marcus, and Helmut Blanke, translators. *The Letter to Philemon: A New Translation with Notes and Commentary.* Grand Rapids, Mich.: William B. Erdmans, 2000.

Baxter, Richard. *The Practical Works of Richard Baxter,* vol. I. London: Henry G. Bohn, 1854.

Bonhoeffer, Dietrich. *Sanctorum Communio: A Theological Study of the Sociology of the Church,* in *Works,* vol. I, edited and translated by Joachim van Soosten. Minneapolis: Fortress Press, 1998.

Boswell, John. *Christianity, Social Tolerance and Homosexuality: Gay People in Western Europe from the Beginning of the Christian Era to the Fourteenth Century.* Chicago and London: University of Chicago Press, 1980.

Braund, Susan, editor. *Lucan: Civil War.* Oxford: Oxford University Press, 1992.

Burnet, Ioannes, editor. *Platonis Opera,* vol. I. Oxford: Oxford University Press, 1904.

———, editor. *Platonis Opera,* vol. III. Oxford: Oxford University Press, 1903.

Campbell, Brian, editor. *The Roman Army 31 BC–AD 337: A Sourcebook.* London and New York: Routledge, 1994.

Cartwright, Christopher. *The Magistrates Authority in Matters of Religion; And the Souls Immortality, Vindicated in two Sermons Preach'd at York.* London: Thomas Underhill, 1647.

Chilton, Bruce. *Rabbi Paul: An Intellectual Biography.* New York: Doubleday, 2004.

Clapp, Theodore. *Slavery: A Sermon, Delivered in the First Congregational Church in New Orleans, April 15, 1838.* New Orleans: J. Gibson, 1838.

Clark, Gillian, editor. *Augustine: Confessions: Book I–IV.* Cambridge: Cambridge University Press, 1995.

Clarke, G. W., translator. *The Octavius of Marcus Minucius Felix.* New York and Ramsey, N.J.: Newman Press, 1974.

Conacher, D. J., editor. *Euripides: Alcestis.* Warminster, Eng.: Aris & Phillips, 1988.

Coogan, Michael D., editor. *The New Oxford Annotated Bible,* 3rd ed. Oxford: Oxford University Press, 1991.

Courtney, E. *A Commentary on the Satires of Juvenal.* London: Athlone Press, 1980.

Crossan, John Dominic. *The Birth of Christianity: Discovering What Happened in the Years Immediately After the Execution of Jesus.* San Francisco: HarperCollins, 1998.

Crossan, John Dominic, and Jonathan L. Reed. *In Search of Paul: How Jesus's Apostle Opposed Rome's Empire with God's Kingdom.* San Francisco: HarperCollins, 2004.

Daly, Mary. *The Church and the Second Sex.* Boston: Beacon Press, 1985.

De Labriolle, Pierre, and François Villeneuve, editors and translators. *Juvénal: Satires.* Paris: Société d'Édition "Les Belles Lettres," 1921.

Dover, K. J. *Greek Homosexuality,* 2nd ed. Cambridge, Mass.: Harvard University Press, 1989.

Edmonds, J. M. *Elegy and Iambus,* vol. I. Cambridge, Mass.: Harvard University Press, 1944.

Eisenbaum, Pamela. "Is Paul the Father of Misogyny and Antisemitism?" *Crosscurrents* (electronic journal), 2001.

Epp, Eldon J., and Gordon D. Fee, editors. *New Testament Textual Criticism: Its Significance for Exegesis: Essays in Honor of Bruce M. Metzger.* Oxford: Clarendon Press, 1981.

Erdkamp, Paul, editor. *A Companion to the Roman Army.* Malden, Mass., Oxford, and Carlton, Australia: Blackwell, 2007.

Fantham, Elaine. *Lucan: De Bello Civili.* Cambridge: Cambridge University Press, 1992.

Farmer, William R., et al., editors. *The International Bible Commentary.* Collegeville, Minn.: Liturgical Press, 1998.

Ferguson, John, editor. *Juvenal: The Satires.* New York: St. Martin's Press, 1979.

Fordyce, C. J., editor. *Catullus: A Commentary,* 2nd ed. Oxford: Clarendon Press, 1965.

Fornaro, Pierpaolo, editor. *Publio Ovidio Nasone: Heroides.* Torino: Edizioni dell'Orso, 1999.

Fowler, Harold North, translator. *Plutarch: Moralia in Fifteen Volumes,* vol. X. Cambridge, Mass.: Harvard University Press, 1960.

Fox, Robin Lane. *Polytheists and Christians.* New York: Alfred A. Knopf, 1987.

Freeman, Derek. *Margaret Mead and Samoa: The Making and Unmaking of an Anthropological Myth.* Cambridge, Mass.: Harvard University Press, 1983.

Gerig, Bruce L. "Homosexuality in the Ancient Near East, Beyond Egypt," in *Homosexuality and the Bible, Supplement 11A,* http://epistle.us/hbarticles/neareast.html, accessed 2005.

Gibson, Roy, editor. *Ovid: Ars Amatoria Book 3.* Cambridge: Cambridge University Press, 2003.

Godwin, John. *Lucretius: De Rerum Natura VI.* Warminster, Eng.: Aris and Phillips, 1991.

Goldsworthy, Adrian, and Ian Haynes, editors. *The Roman Army as a Community.* Portsmouth: R.I.: *Journal of Roman Archaeology,* 1999.

Gomes, Peter. *The Good Book: Reading the Bible with Heart and Mind.* San Francisco: HarperSanFrancisco, 1996.

Gow, A. S., editor. *Theocritus,* 2 vols. Cambridge: Cambridge University Press, 1950.

Greenlee, J. Harold. *Scribes, Scrolls & Scripture: A Student's Guide to New*

Testament Textual Criticism. Grand Rapids, Mich.: William B. Eerdmans, 1985.

Hall, Stuart G. *Doctrine and Practice in the Early Church.* Grand Rapids, Mich.: William B. Eerdmans, 1991.

Halliwell, Stephen, translator. *Aristophanes: Birds, Lysistrata, Assembly-Women, Wealth.* Oxford: Clarendon Press, 1997.

Hine, Daryl, translator. *Puerilities: Erotic Epigrams of the Greek Anthology.* Princeton, N.J., and Oxford: Princeton University Press, 2001.

Hollis, A. S., editor. *Callimachus: Hecale.* Oxford: Clarendon Press, 1990.

The Holy Bible: 1611 Edition. Peabody, Mass.: Hendrickson, 2003.

Hooper, Richard W., translator. *The Priapus Poems: Erotic Epigrams from Ancient Rome.* Urbana and Chicago: University of Illinois Press, 1999.

Hubbard, Thomas K., editor. *Homosexuality in Greece and Rome: A Sourcebook of Basic Documents.* Berkeley and Los Angeles: University of California Press, 2003.

Hude, Carolus, editor. *Lysiae Orationes.* Oxford: Clarendon Press, 1912.

Kenney, E. J., translator. *Apuleius: The Golden Ass.* London: Penguin Books, 1998.

Kenney, E. J., editor. *P. Ovidi Nasonis Amores Medicamina Faciei Femineae Ars Amatoria Remedia Amoris,* 2nd ed. Oxford: Oxford University Press, 1994.

Knox, A. D., and Walter Headlam, editors. *Herodas: The Mimes and Fragments.* Bristol, Eng.: Classical Press, 2001.

Lindsay, W. M., editor. *T. Macci Plauti Comoediae,* vol. 2. Oxford: Clarendon Press, 1905.

Lloyd-Jones, H., and N. G. Wilson, editors. *Sophoclis Fabulae.* Oxford: Clarendon Press, 1990.

Lovering, Eugene H., Jr., and Jerry L. Sumney. *Theology and Ethics in Paul and His Interpreters: Essays in Honor of Victor Paul Furnish.* Nashville: Abingdon Press, 1996.

Mandela, Nelson. *Long Walk to Freedom: The Autobiography of Nelson Mandela.* Boston: Little, Brown, 1994.

Mankin, David, editor. *Horace: Epodes.* Cambridge: Cambridge University Press, 1995.

Marchant, E. C., editor. *Thucydides Book II.* New York: St. Martin's Press, 1966.

———, editor. *Xenophontis Opera Omnia,* vol. 2. Oxford: Clarendon Press, 1921.

Marks, Joseph E., III. *The Mathers on Dancing.* New York: Dance Horizons, 1975.

McBride, Joseph. *Albert Camus: Philosopher and Littérateur.* New York: St. Martin's Press, 1992.

McKeown, J. C., editor. *Ovid: Amores. Text, Prolegomena and Commentary in Four Volumes,* vol. II: *A Commentary on Book One.* Leeds: Francis Cairns, 1989.

McNeal, R. A., editor. *Herodotus: Book I.* Lanham, Md., New York, and London: University Press of America, 1986.

McRay, John. *Paul: His Life and Teaching.* Grand Rapids, Mich.: Baker Academic, 2004.

Mead, Margaret. *Coming of Age in Samoa: A Psychological Study of Primitive Youth for Western Civilization.* New York: William Morrow & Company, 1928.

Meeks, Wayne, et al., editors. *The HarperCollins Study Bible: New Revised Standard Version.* New York: HarperCollins, 1989.

Meeks, Wayne A. *The Writings of St. Paul: A Norton Critical Edition.* New York: W. W. Norton & Company, 1972.

Metzger, Bruce M. *A Textual Commentary on the Greek New Testament,* 2nd ed. Stuttgart: Deutsche Bibelgesellschaft/United Bible Societies, 1994.

Metzger, Bruce M., and Michael D. Coogan. *The Oxford Companion to the Bible.* New York: Oxford University Press, 1993.

Monro, David B., and Thomas W. Allen, editors. *Homeri Opera,* vol. II, *Iliadis Libros XIII–XXIV Continens,* 3rd ed. Oxford: Clarendon Press, 1920.

Morris, Edward P., editor. *Horace: The Satires.* Norman: University of Oklahoma Press, 1939.

Murray, Gilbertus, editor. *Euripidis Fabulae,* vol. I. Oxford: Clarendon Press, 1902.

Mynors, R. A. B., editor. *C. Plini Caecili Secundi Epistularum Libri Decem.* Oxford: Clarendon Press, 1963.

Nestlē, Eberhard and Erwin, et al. *Novum Testamentum Graece,* 5th ed. Stuttgart: Deutsche Bibelgesellschaft, 1998.

Nietzsche, Friedrich. *Beyond Good and Evil: Prelude to a Philosophy and a Future,* 4th ed., translated by Helen Zimmern. London: George Allen & Unwin, 1923.

Nixon, Paul, editor and translator. *Plautus,* vol. III. Cambridge, Mass.: Harvard University Press, 1970.

Page, T. E., editor. *P. Vergili Maronis Bucolica et Georgica.* London and Basingstoke: Macmillan, 1898.

Parker, W. H., editor and translator. *Priapea: Poems for a Phallic God.* London and Sydney: Croom Helm, 1988.

Parshley, H. M., editor and translator. *The Second Sex, Simone de Beauvoir.* New York: Alfred A. Knopf, 1968.

Pelikan, Jaroslav. *Whose Bible Is It? A Short History of the Scriptures.* New York: Penguin, 2005.

Perrin, Bernadotte, translator. *Plutarch's Lives in Eleven Volumes,* vol. VII. Cambridge, Mass.: Harvard University Press, 1958.

———, translator. *Plutarch's Lives in Eleven Volumes,* vol. IV. Cambridge, Mass.: Harvard University Press, 1950.

Postgate, Iohannes Percival, editor. *Tibulli Aliorumque Carminum Libri Tres,* 2nd ed. Oxford: Oxford University Press, 1915.

Powell, J. G. F., editor and translator. *Cicero: Laelius, On Friendship & The Dream of Scipio.* Warminster, Eng.: Aris & Phillips, 1990.

Purser, Ludovicus Claude, editor. *M. Tulli Ciceronis Epistulae,* vol. 1: *Epistulae ad Familiares.* Oxford: Clarendon Press, 1901.

Rackham, H., translator. *Aristotle: Politics.* Cambridge, Mass.: Harvard University Press; London: William Heinemann, 1959.

Rennie, W., editor. *Demosthenis Orationes.* Oxford: Clarendon Press, 1931.

Reynolds, L. D., editor. *C. Sallusti Crispi Catilina, Iugurtha, Historiarum Fragmenta Selecta, Appendix Sallustiana.* Oxford: Clarendon Press, 1991.

———, editor. *L. Annaei Senecae Ad Lucilium Epistulae Morales,* vol. I, *Libri I–XIII.* Oxford: Clarendon Press, 1965.

Rhodes, P. J., editor. *Thucydides History III.* Warminster, Eng.: Aris & Phillips, 1994.

Richlin, Amy. *The Garden of Priapus: Sexuality and Aggression in Roman Humor.* New Haven, Conn.: Yale University Press, 1983.

Rogers, Cleon L., Jr., and Cleon L. Rogers III. *The New Linguistic and Exegetical Key to the Greek New Testament.* Grand Rapids, Mich.: Zondervan, 1998.

Rosenstein, Nathan. *Rome at War: Farms, Families and Death in the Middle Republic.* Chapel Hill: University of North Carolina Press, 2004.

Ruden, Sarah. *Other Places.* Johannesburg, South Africa: Justified Press, 1995.

———, translator. *The Aeneid: Vergil.* New Haven, Conn.: Yale University Press, 2008.

———, translator. *Aristophanes: Lysistrata.* Cambridge, Mass., and Indianapolis: Hackett, 2003.

———, translator. *Homeric Hymns.* Cambridge, Mass., and Indianapolis, Ind.: Hackett, 2005.

———, translator. *Petronius: Satyricon.* Cambridge, Mass., and Indianapolis, Ind.: Hackett, 2000.

Santosuosso, Antonio. *Soldiers, Citizens, and the Symbols of War.* Boulder, Colo.: Westview Press, 1997.

Schönberger, Otto. *Lucius Annaeus Seneca: Apocolocyntosis Divi Claudii.* Würzberg: Königshausen and Neumann, 1990.

Scofield, C. I., et al., editors. *The New Scofield Reference Bible: Holy Bible, Authorized King James Version.* New York: Oxford University Press, 1967.

Sinclair, T. A., editor. *Hesiod: Works and Days.* New York: Arno Press, 1979.

Smith, William, editor. *Dictionary of Greek and Roman Biography and Mythology.* London: Taylor, Walton and Maberly, and John Murray, 1853.

Sommerstein, Alan H., editor and translator. *The Comedies of Aristophanes,* vol. 4: *Wasps.* Warminster, Eng.: Aris & Phillips, 1983.

Stanford, W. B. *The Odyssey of Homer in Two Volumes,* 2nd ed. London and Basingstoke: Macmillan, 1959.

Stickney, Austin, editor. *M. Tulli Ciceronis Cato Maior et Laelius.* New York: Harper and Brothers, 1887.

Stone, I. F. *The Trial of Socrates.* Boston and Toronto: Little, Brown and Company, 1988.

Tarrant, R. J., editor. *P. Ovidi Nasonis Metamorphoses.* Oxford: Clarendon Press, 2004.

Thilo, Georgius. *Servii Grammatici Qui Feruntur in Vergilii Carmina Commentarii,* vol. 2. Hildesheim: Georg Olms, 1961.

Trypanis, C. A., translator. *Callimachus: Aetia, Iambi, Lyric Poems, Hecale, Minor Epic and Elegaic Poems, Fragments of Epigrams, Fragments of Uncertain Location.* Cambridge, Mass.: Harvard University Press, 1958.

Ussher, R. G., editor. *Aristophanes: Ecclesiazusae.* Oxford: Clarendon Press, 1973.

Vaganay, Leon. *An Introduction to New Testament Textual Criticism,* 2nd ed. Cambridge: Cambridge University Press, 1991.

Van Mal-Maeder, D., editor. *Apuleius Madaurensis Metamorphoses.* Groningen: Egbert Forsten, 2001.

Walsh, P. G., translator. *Apuleius: The Golden Ass.* Oxford: Clarendon Press, 1994.

———, editor and translator. *Augustine: De Civitate Dei: Books I & II.* Oxford: Aris & Phillips Classical Texts, 2005.

Walters, Carolus Flamstead, and Robertus Seymour Conway. *Titi Livi Ab Urbe Condita,* vol. 2. *Libri VI–X.* Oxford: Clarendon Press, 1919.

Waltz, Pierre, et al. *Anthologie Grecque: Anthologie Palatine, Tome VIII: Livre IX, Epig. 359–827.* Paris: Société d'Édition "Les Belles Lettres," 1974.

Watson, Lindsay and Patricia, editors. *Martial: Select Epigrams.* Cambridge: Cambridge University Press, 2003.

Weissenborn, W., and H. J. Müller, editors. *Titi Livi Ab Urbe Condita,* 3rd ed. Frankfurt am Main: Weidmann, 1909.

West, M. L., editor. *Iambi et Elegi Graeci ante Alexandrum Cantati,* vol. II. Oxford: Clarendon Press, 1972.

Williams, R. D., editor. *The Aeneid of Vergil: Books 1–6.* London: Macmillan, 1972.

———, editor. *The Aeneid of Vergil: Books 7–12.* London: Macmillan, 1973.

Williams, W. Glynn, translator. *Cicero XXVIII: The Letters to His Friends.* Cambridge, Mass.: Harvard University Press, 1972.

Winter, Bruce W. *Roman Wives, Roman Widows: The Appearance of New Women and the Pauline Communities.* Grand Rapids, Mich., and Cambridge, Eng.: William B. Eerdmans, 2003.

INDEX

A NOTE ON THE TYPE

The text of this book was set in Garamond No. 3. It is not a true copy of any of the designs of Claude Garamond (ca. 1480–1561), but an adaptation of his types, which set the European standard for two centuries. It probably owes as much to the designs of Jean Jannon, a Protestant printer working in Sedan in the early seventeenth century, who had worked with Garamond's romans earlier, in Paris, but who was denied their use because of Catholic censorship. Jannon's matrices came into the possession of the Imprimerie nationale, where they were thought to be by Garamond himself, and were so described when the Imprimerie revived the type in 1900. This particular version is based on an adaptation by Morris Fuller Benton.

COMPOSED BY
Creative Graphics, Allentown, Pennsylvania

PRINTED AND BOUND BY
R. R. Donnelley, Harrisonburg, Virginia

DESIGNED BY
Iris Weinstein